Grounds for Sharing -
a guide to developing special school sites

Jane Stoneham

First published in 1996 by Learning through Landscapes (LTL)

ISBN 1 872865 23 2

Photographs in the book courtesy of the following:

Clare Read, Jane Stoneham, Norma Darey, Len Kerswill, Junko Oikawa, Simon Read, Dini York, Arden School, Chicago Botanic Gardens and LTL.

Book design and production by Steve and Debbie Morrall, LTL/Grafix

Printed in Great Britain by Optimum Litho, Winchester

Acknowledgments

I am very grateful to the following:

The Post Office, the Equitable Charitable Trust, the Frognal Trust and BBC Children in Need, without whom this research could not have been undertaken.

All the special schools which helped with the research by completing the questionnaire and supplying information and photographs. In particular, the schools we visited, where we saw such innovative and inspiring work. The schools included as case studies are from among the many carrying out an exciting range of initiatives throughout the UK.

All the specialist organisations and individuals who gave me advice and, in some cases, commented on the manuscript. These include David Banes, Rosemary Dewar, Barbara Dunne, Kate Kenny, Bill Lucas, Steve Morrall, Caroline Reeves, Liz Russell, Tim Spurgeon, Maggie Walker, Sue Walker and Dr Joan Wood.

Jane Stoneham,
Bath, October 1996

FOREWORD

The Lord Rix
Chairman, Mencap

Many of us would have difficulty describing our school play grounds (and school grounds if any) except in terms of the people we got to know there. The places themselves were often not very inspiring. Indeed, they might still be recalled as threatening by those who associate them with having had to do something energetic and competitive in awful weather, wearing rather skimpy clothing.

Learning through Landscapes has done pioneering work in helping schools to turn even small and unpromising areas into places that are pleasurable, memorable and educational ~ in that order. This has been all the more valuable in neighbourhoods where there are not many breathing spaces, and those there are are neither very pleasant nor very safe.

It is good that the work has moved on to the environments of special schools, catering for children with a range of special needs. Where children are not very mobile, or are impaired in sight or hearing, or have major or generalised learning difficulties, good and imaginative design can literally make a world of difference.

If we learn from children, we can more readily help them to learn: the boy with physical and learning disabilities who likes hanging upside down and making strange noises ~ to see his rather limited world from a different angle, and to attract noises in return; the girl with very limited vision attracted by light reflected from the surface of a pond; the boy who enjoyed the security and predictability of an archway he could feel all round.

To read this book is to see something of a rather special part of their school world through the experience of children who are, as the Children Act would have it, children first and disabled second . . . and very much individuals who are exploring and learning and growing.

CONTENTS

Chapter

INTRODUCTION

1

1.1   Learning through Landscapes and special needs

Learning through Landscapes (LTL) promotes improvements to the educational use and environmental quality of school grounds. To achieve this it coordinates an imaginative programme of activities designed to encourage developments which are long-term and which clearly meet the needs of school communities.

LTL is the only national organisation which specialises in dealing with all aspects of school grounds and, in this respect, is unique in the world. For a number of years it has been concerned to do something to help children in special schools: this book is the result of that concern.

In the latter part of the twentieth century, it is horrifying to think that hundreds of thousands of children with special educational needs spend so much time in entirely inappropriate school grounds. For these young people it is their first sustained experience of a public environment. We are only now just beginning to realise the damage it does to them. Conversely the enormous benefits which developing school grounds can bring is especially true in the special education sector.

In May 1994, Learning through Landscapes began research into special schools with support from the Post Office, the Equitable Charitable Trust, the Frognal Trust and BBC Children in Need. This research was the first of its kind in the UK to look at the design and management of school grounds for children with special needs. The tremendous value of the outdoor environment as an educational resource and as a means of improving the quality of children's lives is now widely recognised and extensively studied by LTL. This book contains guidance which will help to ensure that such benefits are available to all children.

1.2   School grounds and special needs

School grounds can provide an enormous range of opportunities for children with special needs, particularly through an array of sensory stimuli and hands-on experiences. In special education, the division between the formal and informal curriculum is often less well defined. Children learn best through a multi-sensory approach, where social and therapeutic applications play an integral role. Activities in the grounds can simultaneously encourage the development of physical skills, the building of confidence by exploration of the environment and the acquisition of social skills through learning to participate and share with others. The value of school grounds in influencing children's behaviour and encouraging a positive self-image is particularly important. Just as in mainstream education, the hidden curriculum has a potent effect on children with special needs.

Many of the principles involved in designing school grounds apply equally to mainstream and special schools. However there are specific challenges and requirements that need addressing so that developments can offer accessible and stimulating environments for children with special needs. Two key issues highlighted throughout this book are:

* the need for children to have access to a wide range of outdoor interests, and

* the need for them to participate in developments.

A major challenge for many special schools is the wide age range (sometimes stretching from nursery age to school leavers) and the diversity of abilities catered for. Even children within one category of special needs often have quite different individual needs. For example, children with moderate learning difficulties may or may not have associated physical disabilities, sensory impairments, language difficulties or autism. It is therefore essential that the design and management of school grounds are based on an approach that reflects the whole range of identified needs.

Integrating more children with special needs into mainstream schools creates a major challenge. Many buildings and grounds will require extensive modifications to make them fully accessible for children with disabilities. Poor access - narrow doorways, steps and insufficient space in classrooms - can prevent full participation by children who use wheelchairs or mobility aids or have sensory impairments.

School grounds design in a mainstream setting also faces other more subtle challenges. There is a need to consider how to encourage integration between children whose apparent differences can so easily set them apart. Children with special needs are more likely to be bullied and isolated, for example. Such problems obviously need whole-school solutions but there is considerable evidence to suggest that grounds design can play an important role.

1.3   The aims of the book

While some generalisations have been necessary, the overriding aim of this publication has been to show how the development of grounds can help to maximise and encourage abilities and to overcome children's particular challenges. What seems apparent is that the grounds of many schools cater only for a narrow range of outdoor use and therefore fail to address the diverse needs of all children, perhaps especially those with special needs. While it is not possible to give detailed attention to each of these issues in this publication, we hope that the following chapters will highlight some of the ways in which design can help to reduce the dominance of outdoor spaces by small groups and encourage activities that promote better collaboration and understanding.

Throughout the study we found that there is a tremendous amount of support and enthusiasm for developing school grounds for children with special needs, but a lack of written information to back this up. LTL receives numerous enquiries from teachers from special schools, landscape architects and occupational therapists wanting guidance on new projects or to help them make fuller use of the facilities they already have.

This publication attempts to provide advice and information. It is based on our firm conviction that the benefits well-designed and managed school grounds can bring should be available to all children, regardless of age and ability.

It draws on the research undertaken by LTL and the advice of experts in this field of special school grounds.

The advice is intended to be of practical use for special schools wishing to develop and use their sites for a range of purposes.

Advice is presented in the context of a process for developing school grounds which assumes that it will be:

- long-term and sustainable,

- holistic, meeting the needs of some very diverse special school communities, and,

- as participative as possible, involving children with diverse needs with their adult carers wherever possible.

BACKGROUND TO GROUNDS FOR SHARING 2

2.1   The context

In general, although there are books that give detailed guidance on the internal design of buildings for children with special needs, for example, Building Bulletin 77, *Designing for Pupils with Special Educational Needs*, (HMSO) London 1992, the outdoors has received piecemeal attention. Some aspects of the external environment are particularly well served by literature. In particular there is extensive coverage of active uses such as play and sport and hence on aspects of design such as playground and equipment. Organisations such as the Handicapped Adventure Play Association have highlighted the importance of adventure play for disabled children and various organisations now provide advice on play and disability (see 9.5). A range of publications on play deal with issues like access, safety, design of equipment and the opportunities for using play as a therapeutic or creative medium.

There is considerably less information, however, on developing the outdoors as a learning and social resource for children with special needs. *Special Places; Special People* by Wendy Titman, (LTL) highlights the role of landscapes in conveying messages and meanings to children and influencing attitudes and behaviour. Many of the findings apply to children with special needs, but research is needed to look at how some children, especially those with autism or severe learning difficulties, perceive and interact with their environment and the implications for outdoor design. Few studies have involved children with special needs, but a notable exception is *Children's understanding of disability* by Ann Lewis. This book explores the views of children, both children with severe learning difficulties and their non-disabled classmates, on issues such as working together, communication and self-image. One finding that has direct implications for school grounds design is that, in a mixed environment, children with special needs can find outdoor breaks the most traumatic times of the day, associated with bullying and feeling left out.

It is also easier to find literature on certain types of special needs. For example, more books address the needs of children with learning difficulties than children with emotional and behavioural difficulties or autism. While there is good reason why much of the literature on access has addressed the needs of children with physical disabilities and especially wheelchair users, there is a need for more information on the requirements of children with sensory impairments. Some of these are known to be quite different to those of physically disabled children. Different again are the access needs of children with emotional and behavioural difficulties.

Much of the literature addressing technical issues, such as path layout and furniture design, focuses on adults and so the specifications are based on adult sizes. Comprehensive information on the anthropometrics (sizes, shapes and movement patterns) of children who use wheelchairs and different types of mobility aids, and an associated guide to appropriate layouts and space standards, is lacking. Some schools have overcome this by conducting surveys of their children to work out appropriate dimensions.

Certain parallel interest areas have more completely developed the idea of utilising the outdoors for people with special needs. Probably the best example of this is horticultural therapy. This subject was introduced into the UK thirty years ago and is now widely practised with all age groups and types of special needs. With a few exceptions, however, (see 11.9) most of the books are aimed at adults. Some of these texts are no longer in print and can only be obtained through a library.

2.2   Outline of the research

LTL's research included all types of special needs, the whole school age spectrum, residential and non-residential schools and, where possible, mainstream schools. The main aim was to identify appropriate design and management approaches and collect ideas for projects and practical information of use to those planning and implementing school grounds development. A key element of the research was to uncover any existing sources of information and advice and a list of useful books and organisations is included at the end of each chapter to enable people to follow up on areas of particular interest.

The research lasted for two years, during which time contact was made with a large number of special schools, teachers and designers. Questionnaire, interview and site survey techniques were used to explore an enormous range of initiatives already under way. Questionnaires were sent to all special schools and to selected mainstream schools in the UK. 396 questionnaires were returned by schools willing to share their experiences of grounds developments. Detailed analysis was followed by visits to sites across the country which had developed particularly interesting outdoor projects, including some outstanding national examples of good practice. These are described in chapter 14. In addition to this, a group of expert practitioners advised LTL at the outset of the research and at the stage when findings were being written up.

2.3   The research findings

Although we found many examples of successful outdoor projects, many teachers commented that inappropriate design limited the use of the outdoors by children with disabilities. Fortunately much can be done to remove physical barriers and we hope that this book will help to provide some ideas. Social barriers were also highlighted; children with special needs often have fewer opportunities to form relationships, experience success and to take responsibility. Many children with special needs have had limited experience in exploring their environment and this has major implications for the development of mobility skills. They may be withdrawn and apprehensive when facing unfamiliar challenges. School grounds can help by providing motivation, stimulation, encouragement and experience.

The work produced some interesting findings. One of the most significant was the enormous range of special needs and age groups which many special schools cater for. In the questionnaire we asked schools to indicate which categories of special needs were 'dominant' and 'occasional'. We found that many schools have a wide range of different needs to accommodate. The table below shows the breakdown into different categories of the 396 schools.

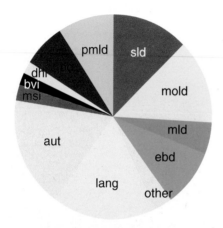

Special Needs Categories: dominant

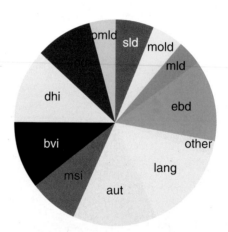

Special Needs Categories: occasional

Key to pie charts	
mld = mild learning difficulties	msi = multi-sensory impairments
mold = moderate learning difficulties	bvi = blind and visual impairments
sld = severe learning difficulties	dhi = deaf and hearing impairments
pmld = profound and multiple learning difficulties	ebd = emotional and behavioural difficulties
aut = autism	lang = language disorders

Nearly half the dominant special needs categories are related to learning difficulties. Some types of special needs, such as physical disabilities, sensory impairments and emotional and behavioural difficulties, do not feature strongly as specific categories but they are often associated with other types of special needs and they do of course place very particular demands on the style and content of the grounds. In this book we have tried wherever possible to make suggestions that are applicable in a wide range of circumstances, but, inevitably, it has been necessary to focus on specific issues from time to time.

It is also common for special schools to cater for a wide age range, in many cases 2-19, and some schools talked of the problems of grounds which fail to provide for the needs of different age groups and the conflicts which can arise from children having to share common facilities.

> "Pupils are most likely to succeed when they are involved in 'doing' activities
> rather than academic learning.
> Environmental education is an ideal activity learning medium."
>
> Barbara Dunne of the Royal Schools for the Deaf in Cheshire

The benefits of developing special school grounds

Above all it was clear from the responses to the questionnaire that the value of school grounds as an educational resource is widely recognised in special education. Teachers highlighted many fundamental benefits that their pupils gain from using the outdoors effectively, as part of both the formal, informal and hidden curriculum. These include:

- improvements in sensory perception, social skills, cooperative skills and work patterns;
- improvements to children's behaviour, especially enabling emotions to be explored more effectively;
- a reduction in aggressive behaviour;
- enhanced learning opportunities outdoors;
- a greater variety of patterns of play, both in a physically demanding, adventurous sense and in the provision of quieter, restful opportunities;
- improvements to the image of the school and to special education in general.

Patterns of use and access

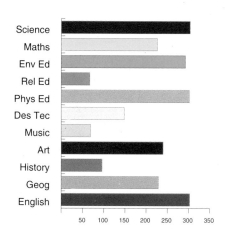

Number of schools using their grounds for different areas of the formal curriculum

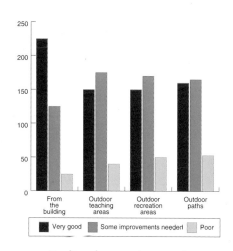

Quality of access in grounds according to schools

The chart (above left) illustrates the use of school grounds in the formal curriculum, showing similar patterns to those in mainstream schools. Distinctions between informal and formal curriculum are less clear in special schools, but it is apparent that the grounds can play an important role in developing social and life skills. Some schools use the grounds as a setting for counselling, having found that many children respond positively to a quiet, relaxed outdoor setting away from the classroom environment. Many schools also find a real value in having safe outdoor areas where children can vent their frustrations with little risk of injuring themselves or others.

An overriding issue for all schools is to make sure that the grounds can be reached easily and safety by all children. Almost half the schools said they had some problems with inadequate access, particularly for children with physical disabilities (including wheelchair users), profound and multiple learning difficulties or visual impairments. Most problems related to access within the school grounds, rather than from the building and the majority of these could be solved by adaptations if resources were available. The chart (above right) summarises these findings.

Needs

The examples in this book have all been successfully implemented by schools throughout the UK. They show that despite the lack of research support, teachers have explored and resolved many of the particular issues that determine whether children with special needs have the opportunity to use and enjoy the outdoors. The chapter which follow provide advice in the areas of need identified during the research

> "There are immense benefits in developmental terms for our client group.
> Students grow up personally, socially and culturally".
>
> N De Reybekill of Handsworth Alternative School in Birmingham

PLANNING & MANAGING CHANGE

3

Adequate planning of school grounds improvements is essential to ensure that they serve the whole school community. Piecemeal developments often fail to address the most important needs in the school and can easily result in an unrealistic workload for one or two people. The lack of an overall plan can also make it harder to get funding, to receive agreement from the headteacher or to inspire other people to get involved. Even in special schools it is possible to involve many pupils in the planning and development of changes as well as later on.

3.1 Strategy for grounds development

Research into good practice in mainstream primary schools has enabled Learning through Landscapes to develop a sequence of critical steps. This research into special schools has shown that a very similar process has been adopted by special schools for which it forms a useful structure or plan. The chart below shows how the process has been explored in this book. It is important to note that the stages need to be seen as a guide and used flexibly.

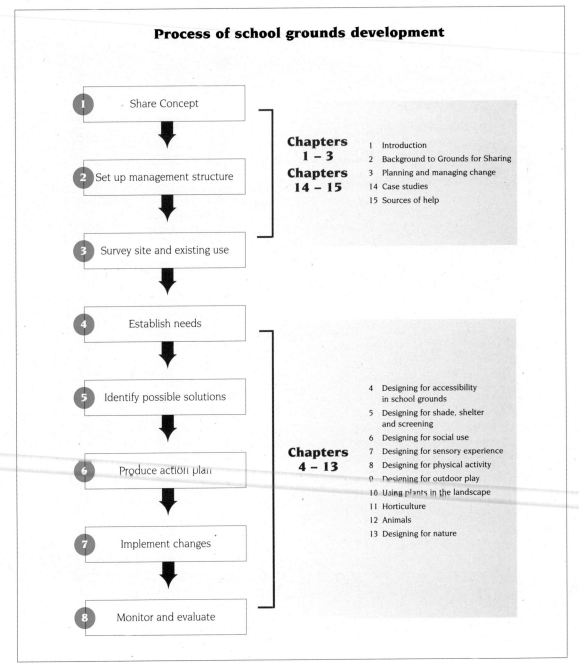

Process of school grounds development

1. Share Concept
2. Set up management structure
3. Survey site and existing use
4. Establish needs
5. Identify possible solutions
6. Produce action plan
7. Implement changes
8. Monitor and evaluate

Chapters 1 – 3
Chapters 14 – 15

1. Introduction
2. Background to Grounds for Sharing
3. Planning and managing change
14. Case studies
15. Sources of help

Chapters 4 – 13

4. Designing for accessibility in school grounds
5. Designing for shade, shelter and screening
6. Designing for social use
7. Designing for sensory experience
8. Designing for physical activity
9. Designing for outdoor play
10. Using plants in the landscape
11. Horticulture
12. Animals
13. Designing for nature

a) Sharing the idea

The first step involves communicating ideas to others so as to get the agreement and support of the headteacher, other teachers, other staff including therapists, parents and governors. Presentations, videos, displays, meetings and handouts are ways of sharing the benefits of grounds development. A talk from a visiting speaker, for example from a special school which has carried out successful school grounds developments or from a member of staff of the local education authority, can often be a successful way of drawing attention to the possibilities and demonstrating outside support for your ideas.

An example of a display made by a school to promote sharing of ideas.

b) Setting up a management structure

There are many different aspects that need to be considered when planning special school grounds developments. Setting up a management structure for the project will help share the work load, allow individuals' expertise to be matched to particular tasks and should result in a more efficient and effective approach. Major areas to be addressed are likely to include fundraising, different areas of the curriculum, access, information dissemination (newsletter, assemblies etc), and social policies (bullying, interaction etc). A named co-ordinator is often helpful as there is a particularly wide range of external agencies in special schools which may need to be involved. Most special schools find that a small management group on which the headteacher, a teacher, another specialist member of staff and a parent/governor sits is an appropriate structure. In some cases it is helpful to include one or two representatives of outside agencies.

c) Evaluating existing provision

Before deciding on any improvements, it will be necessary to be fully aware of existing resources, what is there, how it is being used and how it could better serve children and staff.

- A site plan will be essential, probably obtainable from the local education authority and it will need to be enlarged to a workable scale (anything smaller than 1:200 is difficult to use). Ideally this will show not only the obvious features such as buildings and roads but hidden obstacles such as the layout of service cables and pipes and positions of existing trees and shrub belts. Much additional information about the elements you already have on site will need to be added.

- Legal, technical, safety guidelines and school policy documents are required. Key LEA contacts, advisers, local organisations and possible sources of funds or materials will need to be identified.

- Assessments of the quality and appropriateness of the existing access throughout the school grounds and to different activities and facilities (water, gardening, wildlife etc) will need to be made as well as patterns of site use, which routes are used, where cars are parked and where deliveries are made.

- Identification of existing hazards, such as dangerous equipment, broken paving and steep slopes can be undertaken at this stage.

- Above all a clear picture of how the grounds are currently being used in both the formal and informal curriculum is necessary alongside observations of the more subtle ways in which the site is affecting children.

- Any behavioural and social problems such as bullying, isolation of some children, lack of cohesion or integration and vandalism should be noted at this stage.

- A thorough examination of the way in which maintenance is carried out, how flexibly it is operated, how much it costs and any specific aspects relating to the safety of ramps, etc. Some of this basic survey work can be undertaken by pupils, especially those elements relating to their opinions of current site use. Adults working closely with particular children may be able to help articulate their views.

d)   Establishing needs

It is important to look at current patterns of use.

It is also important to look at access to features such as ponds.

This is a particularly important part of the process where the needs of the whole special school community need to be identified. There are many factors to consider and doing so will require the input of a large number of individuals (pupils, staff, helpers, parents, governors, visitors). In particular the following information needs to be established:

- what teachers want to be able to teach outside in the formal curriculum being delivered;

- what children want to be able to do during break times. In residential schools this will require much fuller exploration;

- what teachers and other staff, parents, governors, and day-time supervisors want the children to get from the grounds;

- what other uses the grounds should support, for example events and shared site use by other local groups;

- what use is made of the grounds by other schools or outside groups;

- the image of the school and how it might be presented to the school and its wider community.

Exploring these issues will depend on involving as many different groups and individuals as possible. It is particularly useful to become more aware of how children value the grounds and what changes they would like to see. This may be difficult with children who find it hard to communicate or to express themselves but may be possible through the use of prompting materials such as pictures, symbols or videos. Children can be involved in conducting surveys, for example, to identify reachable heights for wheelchair-users or successful colour contrasts and text sizes for those with visual impairments. The act of asking children and listening and watching for views can also help them to feel more involved and to realise that they can have an influence.

e) Identifying possible solutions

Once needs have been identified and a list of possible ways of meeting them have been drawn up, the most appropriate solutions for the school can be identified. This must take into account the information collected about the site as it is now. Outside help may be particularly appropriate at this stage and may include advice from other schools, the LEA, designers and organisations specialising in special needs and school grounds. It is important to be clear about how any outside agent is to help and what costs will be involved before engaging them.

It is important to relate preferred solutions to the school's development plan, policy documents and management structures to ensure that they are achievable and that there are no legal, technical or maintenance problems. Once agreed, the proposals can be used for fund raising, for communicating the final plans to others and for organising site works.

f) Producing a school grounds action plan

It is unlikely that schools will be able to, or want to, implement all the changes immediately. Instead developments can be phased into different stages. This can have several advantages; it gives the fund raising smaller individual targets, allows more continuous involvement of children and makes it easier to adjust the pace of work to match the abilities of the children.

It is important to prioritise proposed changes so that each phase can be dealt with appropriately. This may have to be largely dictated by technical issues, such as access for large construction machinery or by financial implications, such as the donation of certain materials. Funding, too, may have to be used in a certain timescale. On the other hand there may be clear priorities relating to the needs of children or staff, for example the need for improved access or removal of hazards. Once identified, the phased development should be outlined on a plan and final permission, if required, should be obtained from the relevant authorities.

g) Implementing changes

The decision as to how to implement plans will depend on the nature of the changes involved, available finance and access to sources of skilled voluntary help. Detailed designs and specifications may be needed so that the work is clearly outlined. It must also be clear how children are likely to be involved at each stage.

It will be necessary to identify sources of appropriate materials, labour and equipment. Other schools, the LEA and the designer (if you are employing one) will be able to help with this. Where possible the skills of staff, governors and parents need to be incorporated and children involved. If the work is to be carried out by volunteers insurance cover may be needed and the work may have to be checked to make sure it meets safety standards. The LEA will be able to advise on this.

Involving children in the early stages of construction.

Before and after photographs are an excellent way of recording change.

After: Alley now developed into secret play area for infants.

h) Monitoring and evaluating changes

Setting up a system to monitor and evaluate changes made will help schools to reflect upon and celebrate achievements. It is also inevitable that circumstances will change over time and plans may need to be adjusted to meet different needs, for example, as staff and pupils change. Photographs are an excellent means of recording some aspects of change, but it may well be that specialist agencies working with your school will be able to quantify behavioural and attitudinal improvements in pupils as a result of developments.

Provision needs to be made for feedback from staff, pupils and all others who have been involved. This can be done by regular meetings, visits to other schools to look at different approaches and possibilities, the additional comments to a development plan and through in-service training sessions.

3.2   Common issues

Sites

Many special schools occupy buildings and land designed for other purposes. There may be aspects of the previous use of a site which will be particularly important to change. Equally, there may be features which can be easily adapted or incorporated such as hedgerows, exotic trees, ridges and furrows, dove cotes, etc. Old photographs, maps, documents and newspapers will help to give an insight into this. They are normally available from a local library or local history group.

Local climate and the existence of shelter on site will influence the way children can use the space: in most cases more shelter will be desirable. Vulnerability to cold winds and sun will need to be borne in mind. In special schools it will be particularly important to select areas with appropriate microclimates for different uses such as seating, play and gardening areas.

The topography of a special school's grounds will, inevitably be important. Sloping sites may constrain access, particularly for children with limited mobility. In these cases design solutions which enable as much of the area as possible to be opened up to children will be most helpful. For example, modifications through earth moving and retaining walls to create more level areas and acceptable gradients on paths. Slopes over a long distance are particularly difficult for some children to manage.

Often it will be important to look especially closely at patterns of pedestrian and vehicular access. If at all possible, they need to be separated. In some cases management solutions such as limited or controlling access to certain parts of the site may need to be considered. Access issues are explored in more detail in Chapter 4.

New schools will inevitably have problems of soil compaction and debris as a result of building works and there may need to be remedial works such as deep cultivation and rubbish removal. Contaminants in the soil, such as broken glass or pollutants will be particularly important if children are to be involved in planting and digging. Soil type (pH, fertility and texture) will have a major influence on horticulture programmes. (see Chapter 11.)

Drainage patterns will influence the use of the grounds. For example, poorly drained grass areas may be inaccessible to wheelchairs users for a significant period and paths in boggy areas will only be fine-weather routes.

Existing underground and overhead services will need to be identified before site construction is undertaken. Additional services are more often required in special schools. For example, water and electricity to a horticulture project or heating for out-buildings.

It is important to be aware of any legal conditions that may influence site works. For example, access standards for wheelchair users. Public Rights of Way, Tree Preservation Orders, Conservation Areas, Sites of Special Scientific Interest (or other conservation designations). The local authority will be able to advise on this. Neighbours will need to be informed of plans to plant trees or erect buildings and fences near their properties.

A significant factor will be the presence of local environmental resources which are accessible to pupils including local mainstream schools. Those which have developed programmes for children with special education needs are of obvious use. They may also have staff whose skills can be utilised by a special school developing its grounds. In almost all cases projects are enriched when they involve the local community.

More detailed information about such matters as shelter, access, drainage, legal issues and all the other matters which affect all school site developments, can be obtained from LTL.

3.3   Structuring the landscape

School grounds typically lack structure and instead are characterised by expanses of grassland and asphalt.

A main consequence is that outdoor areas are open to the extremes of cold winds, rain and sun, with serious implications for children who require more protection. Many schools also complain of the unstructured way in which such grounds are used and how boisterous, physical activities easily dominate and prevent some children finding quiet areas for passive pursuits.

Successful grounds design relies on careful structuring of the landscape so as to create opportunities for different uses and for the more positive benefits associated with good grounds development such

An expanse of asphalt being "broken up" by wooden structures.

as stimulation, interest, anticipation and variety. This relies particularly on the creation of shelter and shade (see chapter 5), and on the creation of a range of spaces within the site and the use of structure planting (see chapter 10). A key principle is always to find solutions which meet the maximum number of needs.

3.4   Planning for the participation of children with special needs

It is important to involve children working with adults as much as possible in all stages of a project, from its initial planning through to ongoing maintenance. This will help extend options within the formal curriculum and will have benefits for children's social development. In particular it will foster responsibility, self-esteem, greater interest and an ability to work as part of a team.

However, there are some particular challenges for special schools associated with this approach. Involving children at any stage may lead to more work for staff but will have positive benefits in staff/pupil relationships. There will be a need to plan activities and to identify ways in which children can safely participate without disrupting work schedules and contract deadlines. Some stages of the developments may simply be too dangerous or under too much pressure of time to be considered but most will offer a range of interesting possibilities. It will always be important to have an excellent grasp of pupils' capabilities.

Making a hedgehog box.

There are some obvious challenges when trying to enable children with profound disabilities to participate in some stages in more than a token way. This is likely to be most difficult with construction and maintenance work which requires a wide range of physical skills. For schools catering for pupils with a limited ability range this can lead to problems when applying for funding if there is a stipulation for a level of pupil involvement which cannot be met. Funding organisations are becoming more aware of the problem and may take this into account when looking at grant applications.

Involving children in the early stages of project planning is an excellent way of introducing them to the idea of environmental improvements and making it clear that they can play an active part. It is obviously important to present information to the children in a form that they can understand and it may be appropriate to prepare a simple, sketch plan which includes pictures, symbols and text that they can relate to. Symbols of such features as seats, trees and ponds can be moved around a plan and give children the chance to try out different ideas. Doing some site work, such as taking pictures, surveying or clearing areas, will help familiarise children with the area and will show them that things are progressing. Preparing a diary will also help children see that they are making progress and can include all types of curriculum work.

If children are to be involved in construction work it is important not to over-estimate their pace of work, especially if they are doing activities they are not familiar with or using skills that are especially difficult for them. Sufficient time needs to be allowed for this phase and, if contractors are involved, flexible ways of involving the children needs to be considered. For example, some schools have included a clause in the contract specification which says that children are to be able to participate in certain tasks, such as planting, or spreading a bark mulch. Another approach has been to get contractors to leave some areas clear for children to finish themselves. Whatever the approach, all parties involved must be well informed and invited to discuss any problems they foresee. In some cases specially-designed tools can be made.

Some schools have successful working relationships with landscape architects and other professionals who plan and develop projects in collaboration with pupils. This may involve setting up a management structure comprised of pupils and developing a system whereby they are able to manage the project with help from staff only as and when needed. Such a working arrangement can be a new experience for the landscape architect, who must be fully briefed beforehand.

Maintenance offers a wide range of activities to children but there can be special challenges in trying to fit in with existing management systems. This is discussed in more detail in 3.6.

The final stages of building a pond.

3.5   Planning for maintenance

Schools which embark on the development of their grounds to provide a rich resource for pupils must ensure high standards of safety and minimum maintenance demands. Often schools are able to raise capital money for investment into a grounds project, but the maintenance has to be achieved within existing budget constraints. It is therefore important to consider the maintenance implications of grounds improvements early in the planning stage. If work is being done by a professional designer, it is worth getting them to prepare a maintenance plan. This will help the school to plan for future maintenance and will also make sure that the designer has given this sufficient consideration.

Maintenance includes activities that are not physically demanding.

Clearly schools will wish to minimise unnecessary maintenance costs, but the easiest grounds to maintain are usually those which are also the least exciting. Ideally maintenance should not be seen just as a costly chore; in many cases it is possible to see the work as a positive part of a process that cares for the environment or brings the landscape design to fruition. Many of the activities that must be carried out can be incorporated into both the formal and informal curriculum.

Nevertheless within the framework of desired activity, careful attention to design and to management systems can minimise the extent to which maintenance becomes an impossible burden on resources. Unfortunately much of the advice usually given about 'low maintenance' landscapes takes a rather simplistic approach that equates low maintenance with a reduction in regular attention. To fully assess maintenance demand, the work inputs into the grounds need to be considered in the light of the skills, resources and effort required and the way that patterns of input are required through the year.

Closely mown grass, for example, is cheap to establish but needs regular attention throughout the growing season. However, this work can often be quickly and easily done. Other styles of landscape design traditionally referred to as low maintenance, such as ground cover plantings, need capital investment and a high standard of attention in the establishment period before any cost savings begin to materialise.

Another contrast is seen in wildlife gardens or ecological areas. These may need little attention through the year, but periodically require skilled management decision making and every so often very large labour intensive inputs. Usually these areas require a completely different range of maintenance equipment.

The decision of which style represents 'low maintenance' therefore depends on the choice of maintenance system and the level of involvement that the school wishes to adopt. For more detailed description of grounds maintenance systems, refer to A *guide to the management and maintenance of school grounds*, Joan Wood and Michael Littlewood, (LTL, 1996).

3.6   Involving children in maintenance

It is desirable to involve children in grounds maintenance as much as possible. Children with special needs often have limited opportunity to take responsibility and looking after parts of their school environment can help to foster feelings of involvement and accomplishment. It can also help to instill respect for the environment and to make them see that they can have a positive effect on the world around them. However it is equally important that they are not given tasks which are too challenging, since the negative effects of failure are clearly undesirable.

Identifying maintenance tasks that are to be the responsibility of teachers and pupils therefore needs careful consideration, and this is particularly so where children with special needs are members of the team. Tasks should be chosen that are within the range of physical skills and resources available. Tasks that have to be

Taking part in maintenance can help foster feelings of involvement and achievement.

frequently repeated, such as grass mowing, are usually less feasible (and less popular) than infrequent tasks which lead to dramatic changes (such as clearing hay from a wildflower meadow). Special tools and equipment will make tasks more manageable (see 11.6)

Schools also have many other demands on their time, some of which may be unexpected or difficult to plan for. Most also have times when staff and pupils are not there. The ideal maintenance tasks for participation are therefore those which have a high degree of flexibility in timing. If a job is time critical and the consequences of not doing it moderately serious then it should be tackled professionally through contract maintenance or some other maintenance system.

3.7   Planning for safety

Maintenance performs many functions within a landscape, but one of the most important is to ensure that the grounds and the features within them remain safe for use. It is not possible to achieve a totally safe environment and children will always find ways to take risks. It is therefore a case of trying to make things as safe as reasonably possible while creating an environment that children want to use.

Many aspects of safety are wide ranging and influence other decisions in the grounds improvement process. These are therefore discussed in other sections of this publication. For example the layout of the grounds is important. Inadequate circulation space may result in accidents from children crashing into each other. Poor division between different types of space, especially between active and passive uses and between pedestrian and bicycle routes may also increase accident frequency. Safety aspects of plants, and particularly of potentially toxic plants, are also discussed later.

Schools that are based in properties that were originally designed for a different use, such as a former house or a building for a different category of special needs, can experience particular problems with landscape features which are not sufficiently robust, poor access or possible hazards such as ornamental ponds. Various schools have shown how school grounds developments can be achieved to overcome many of these problems (see chapter 14).

Maintaining safety relies on:

- a clear policy on required standards;
- good monitoring and adequate supervision to ensure standards are maintained;
- responsive maintenance systems that can get work done quickly.

Maintenance requirements and the safety of furniture and hard materials are strongly dictated by decisions in the design and construction stage. Choosing robust materials that have a long life with minimal maintenance demand may cost more initially, but in the long run will be cheaper than materials that require constant repair or replacement. Construction techniques should ensure that features are strong, safe and long-lasting. For example, wood joints are stronger if screwed or bolted than if they are nailed.

Many schools rely on community involvement or volunteer workers to get projects done. If volunteers are used it is important to ensure suitably high standards of construction so that the work will pass health and safety requirements.

3.8   Monitoring school grounds

In some schools on-site maintenance staff such as the caretaker have responsibility for monitoring the grounds. This is obviously not possible in schools where maintenance is carried out entirely by outside contractors. The most successful systems tend to involve the whole school in the monitoring process. The spirit to foster is that it is everyone's responsibility to keep an eye on the grounds and to note any problems which need attention. However it is also important that one person has responsibility for periodic checks as a safeguard.

There are some aspects of the school grounds which will require particular attention notably access provision and play equipment. Checks should look at the following:

Paths and hard surfaces

- Deterioration of materials (cracks, pot holes, loose and uneven slabs etc).
- Algal growth which is making them slippery.
- Encroachment of adjacent plants (especially brambles or branches at eye level).
- Litter and debris (including slippery leaves, glass, gravel etc).

Play equipment

- Bolts and connections.
- Weight-supporting surfaces.
- Loosening joints.
- Splinters and rough edges.
- Impact absorption of safety surfaces.
- Topping up and forking over of loose surfaces such as bark.

Many aspects of safety management can be incorporated into a routine or contract maintenance system, but there will also be times when unforeseen events require that specific contracts or work requests are issued. Once problems are identified it is usually important that one person has responsibility for implementing action so that there is no ambiguity of responsibility.

3.9   Sources of information

References

Special Places; Special People, Wendy Titman, LTL, 1994

Children's understanding of disability, Ann Lewis, 1995, Routledge, London

Organisations

Learning through Landscapes, 3rd Floor, Southside Offices, The Law Courts, Winchester SO23 9DL

Remember that access can change as plants grow.

DESIGNING FOR ACCESSIBILITY

4

4.1 Introduction

Good access is essential to ensure that all children have maximum chance to use and enjoy the outdoors. Poor access results in denied opportunities, increased risks of accidents and enforced dependency on others. The current trend towards greater integration of children with special needs into mainstream schools makes it important for all schools to adopt a policy of universal access. However the greatest challenges can be associated with situations where the varying requirements of many different groups of special needs children have to be integrated together. It is also the case that individual children may exhibit more than one type of disability. Allowance may have to be made in the design for the construction of supporting environments that strike a balance between many different needs. Often it is the needs of children who are semi-ambulant and those who use wheelchairs which dictate the most substantial design modifications. The majority of the guidelines given in this chapter therefore relate to situations where such needs have to be accommodated.

4.2 Designing for different needs

The priority is to design entrances, outdoor paths and hard surfaces to accommodate as full a range of special needs as possible and to ensure that children are not denied access to any of the opportunities and activities which the site offers. Designing for accessibility involves consideration of the whole site layout as well as of details of construction. For example, it may not be realistic to make all areas of the school grounds fully accessible or it may be that a less direct route will overcome difficult topography. It is essential to make sure that the most frequently used features are in the most accessible locations. Distance is also an important consideration for children with limited stamina and there should be things of interest in the school grounds which are near to the school building. It is also the case that children with limited mobility, or who are frail, may require more protected areas during cold, damp and hot weather.

Access to teaching resources such as trees.

For children with mobility challenges, surfaces for paths and hard areas should be firm, even-surfaced and non-slip; loose materials such as gravel are inappropriate. Gravel is also totally unsuitable for children with emotional and behavioural difficulties. The Table on pages 28 - 29 summarises the advantages and disadvantages of different materials which can be used for path and hard area construction.

Sometimes steps and slopes are deliberately provided as a challenge to children with physical disabilities, to enable them to learn to deal with these features in the outside world or to develop particular gross motor skills. It is not advisable to build these into the main access routes but to incorporate them into minor routes where children have alternatives to reach a particular destination.

Blind children rely on tactile cues to find their way around the environment. Children with some residual sight may be able to see contrasts and it can be helpful if kerbs or edgings are a different colour to the path surface. Step nosings should be highlighted with a contrasting material to give both visual and textural indicators. Changes in path surface texture at the approach to hazards such as steps, ramps and junctions help to provide warnings. Textures included in paths and hard surfaces can also be used to indicate direction. Kerbs can be an important aid to direction finding or to mark the location of a feature.

Deaf children may be able to pick up visual cues but will not respond to aural warnings and so it is important to consider any hazards which are a risk to them. For example, if paths are to be shared with wheeled traffic it is important to clearly identify pedestrian-only zones.

Imaginative use of hard materials to give interesting colour and texture effects.

Textured strips are particularly valuable for children with sensory impairments.

In many schools there is a problem of accidents from children crashing into one another on crowded playgrounds. This is particularly serious for children who bruise easily or have fragile bones. Creating quieter areas, where boisterous play is barred, is important for these children along with those who welcome an alternative to running around or playing football. The use of soft surfaces can be a sensible measure for children with fragile bones. Children with limited spatial awareness and/or learning difficulties may need extra supervision to ensure they do not cause accidents.

Grass areas are often too wet for children to go on during the winter. Particularly for children with limited mobility or who use wheelchairs. It is therefore sensible to plan hard areas which can be used as alternatives at such times.

Obviously it can be hard to generalise about the full range of requirements for design of a special needs or integrated school. Nevertheless the following broad guidelines should be of value in identifying the main areas of consideration.

4.3   The school entrance

The safe arrival and departure of children is a fundamental issue for any school and although little can be done about the nature of the public space outside the school gates, it is important that the school site itself offers safe and convenient access. Where space permits, it is good policy to separate vehicular and pedestrian access so that children do not have to walk between cars and buses, a particularly hazardous exercise for wheelchair users who cannot so easily be seen by drivers. Footpaths need to be sufficiently wide to cater for the large numbers of children using them at the start or end of the school day. If possible locate parking areas away from the school entrance and limit vehicular access near the building to 'dropping off' and ambulance/emergency access only.

4.4   Indoor - outdoor

Good outdoor access starts with the building; children must be able to get outside easily if they are to have the freedom to use the school grounds. Ideally there will be access from each classroom. Sufficiently wide doorways (minimum 900mm) with an absence of step or threshold and with doors which are easy to open are all basic requirements for children with limited mobility and wheelchair users. Doors which require a lot of pressure to open are difficult for children with limited strength. Also, handles which are stiff or awkward need to be avoided. Including an extra door latch which is out of reach of the children and which can be operated at the discretion of staff will make it possible to control access.

4.5   Controlling access

Of course there are times when it is necessary to prevent access. This will rely on a whole range of school policies for supervision but the design of the grounds will play an important role. Many teachers emphasise the importance of open spaces for children to be able to run around and to have maximum freedom. This requires attention to safety aspects such as adequate boundaries to ensure that children cannot run out onto nearby roads or into no-go areas such as car parks. Internal boundaries will also be important to create

Wide, firm, even surfaced paths ensure access for all children.

different areas and to give teachers the option of limiting access to particular areas when necessary. Shrubs and climbers can help soften fences and walls and in some situations it may be possible to use hedges as internal boundaries.

4.6 Paths

Main access paths should be firm, even-surfaced and non-slip. In many cases they will need to accommodate all types of disability although there may be a focus on one in particular, for example visual impairments. There may be a wide variety of use, from walking and wheelchair use to riding bikes and carts.

Appropriate path widths will depend on the likely volume and frequency of use but they should at least accommodate a single wheelchair.

The layout and design of routes will be influenced primarily by the topography. It may be necessary to grade different routes according to how challenging they are, and to provide a choice of directions or cut-backs so that children with less stamina can still follow a short walk through landscape. The construction of regular 'goals' and resting points, preferably associated with views or some other reason to linger, is desirable.

A useful exercise is to identify a hierarchy of routes through the school grounds. It is important to note which paths will be the main access routes and which must accommodate busy and frequent use. Secondary paths are those which receive lighter use and which therefore need not be as wide but which may still need to make allowance for people moving in small groups or passing each other. Minor paths may be routes which are designed to allow for single-file access. It is almost as important not to over-design paths as to make poor provision for access, since excessively large paths can destroy interest and make an area look institutional, as well as eat excessively into budgets. An alternative way to provide interest is to vary the path width, as long as a minimum width is maintained throughout. Take care to consider which routes children are likely to take through the grounds and plan paths accordingly; if there is a short cut across the grass, children are likely to use it with the result of a worn 'desire line'.

Use materials which are in keeping with the setting. The table at the end of this section summarises the main choices. For main paths it is best to use materials which are hard wearing and which require minimal maintenance. If you choose tarmac, asphalt or concrete, consider ways of improving their appearance.

In more natural areas of the landscape the challenge is to make paths accessible without destroying the character of the surroundings. Asphalt and in-situ concrete are too harsh in their raw state but can be dressed with a binding layer of chippings to create an attractive and functional surface. Self-binding gravel

Paintings on tarmac provide a series of coloured routes.

Sculpture and colour combine to create a stimulating sensory design.

Natural materials and plants create a restful sensory trail.

or wood chippings (if of suitable construction - see Table on pages 28 - 29) are options but will be prone to waterlogging and rutting in damp areas and during wet weather so may not be the best choice for all-weather access. Earth or grass paths can be tolerated for some special needs groups, but may still restrict access to the best weather conditions and can easily deteriorate into mud.

There is often little opportunity for extensive modification of topography. Where steep slopes or side cambers are unavoidable the provision of handrails, kerbs, resting places and seats becomes of even more importance. Regular maintenance is important. Ensure there are no overhanging branches and remember that it is particularly hard for blind people to detect obstacles above waist height. Even for children with mild visual impairment low level hazards such as brambles may also be hard to see when the path is enclosed and shaded. It is also important to keep the paths in good repair, since for semi-ambulant or wheelchair using children it may be impossible to move off the path to avoid a problem area.

A rope trail provides a simple and effective woodland guide for children with visual impairments.

PATH DETAILS	
Width	Main routes: 1.8m (2 wheelchairs can pass) Secondary routes: 1.2m (1 wheelchair with passing space for pedestrian)
Minor routes:	900mm min. (single wheelchair)
Passing places	Provide these on paths which are 1.2m wide or less.
Junctions	Provide warnings on approach to junctions with roads and busy paths. Textured strips are useful for children with visual impairments and the width of these can be sequenced to indicate the approach to hazards.
Clearance	Ensure adequate space between the path and obstacles, such as signs, trees etc. Also make allowance for obstacles on paths near buildings, particularly windows which open outwards.
Camber	Maximum cross fall on a path: 1:50. Preferred: 1:100.

4.7 Interpretation, signage

Many special needs children experience difficulties with communication, either as a consequence of learning difficulties or as a side-effect of some other characteristic, such as hearing loss. Signs, interpretative features and warnings therefore have to provide information in simple, clear ways, using pictorial, textural and colour coded information as alternatives or additions to text. In schools which use symbol communication systems such as Makaton or Rebus, these can be used throughout the grounds. Braille is useful for those blind children who can read it. For those who

A tactile relief map.

can't, recorded messages and textural methods such as raised maps, moon symbols and shapes should be considered. Children with some residual sight may be able to read text as long as the lettering is sufficiently large and in strong contrast to the background.

Blind or visually impaired children will rely more on tactile information for wayfinding and using different textures for different routes can help. Also provide landmarks which help children to distinguish different areas of the grounds, such as groups of white stemmed birch, information boards and sculptures. If there are steps make sure that children

An imaginative way of providing tactile information: a miniature replica of a Zen garden.

have warnings on approach (include texture strips) and ensure that the step edges are clearly contrasted. In natural areas there can be far fewer cues for self-orientation. Formal and informal interpretation and location aids are therefore required.

4.8 Ramps, slopes and steps

Ramps are essential for wheelchair users and for children who find steps difficult or unnerving. But ramps are a problem for many semi-ambulant children and can be more hazardous, especially when wet. They should therefore be designed to complement steps rather than to replace them. The technical requirements for ramps and steps are outlined below but it is also important to consider aesthetics. Ramps, steps and handrails can look harshly functional and place an unnecessary focus on disability and 'special environments'. Consider ways of softening these features by choosing attractive materials in keeping with the surroundings, giving good attention to detailing and including plants alongside.

A tactile sculpture including poems written in Braille.

Symbols incorporated into a sensory design.

RAMP, SLOPE AND STEP DETAILS

Gradient	Consider gradient together with distance; long ramps at even a slight gradient can be very tiring and sometimes a shorter, steeper ramp may be preferable. A 1:15 gradient is often the maximum that can be managed comfortably, but there may be a need for this to be reduced to 1:20 where long distances are unavoidable.
Length	The maximum distance even at the gentlest gradient should be 10m. Longer ramps should have resting platforms at a maximum of 10m distance apart.
Low edging kerbs/rails	Incorporate low kerbs or rails, at least 40mm high, along each side.
Handrails	Provide handrails or supports on both sides and extend them at least 500mm beyond the top and bottom of the ramp.
Approaches	Ensure a clear area of at least 1.5m length at top and bottom approaches.Use textured surfaces on approaches to provide warnings to visually disabled children.
Steps	All steps in a series should be of the same dimensions. Maximum rise of a series: 1.2m. Avoid single steps (especially shallow ones) as these can easily be overlooked. If you must have a single step, use a contrasting material or colour to highlight it (see below).
Treads & risers	Tread: minimum 280mm. Riser: maximum 150mm.
Approaches	Use textured surfaces on approaches to provide warnings to visually disabled children.
Nosings	Ensure good contrast to highlight individual steps. Use contrasting materials or paint to highlight step nosings.
Handrails	Provide handrails or supports on both sides and extend them at least 500mm beyond the top and bottom of the flight.

4.9   Bridges and fords

The design and construction of bridges obviously depends very much on the nature and the width of the feature to be crossed, the likely traffic the bridge must support and the budget available. Many opportunities exist to make bridges an exciting component of the landscape, giving a strong and elegant visual focus, or providing a chance to stop and look at views or water beneath. The following guidelines are therefore the minimum that are required to provide an accessible structure.

An accessible and attractive bridge.

This bridge has removable rails so that children can have direct access to the water.

Fords enable children to experience the sensation of splashing through water. It is important to choose a functional and durable material. Concrete is a good choice but ensure that the surface is textured to make it non-slip. Semi-ambulant children may need a handrail.

BRIDGE DETAILS

Gradient	Ideally, bridges should be constructed level with the surrounding paths. Where they have to be raised (to accommodate traffic passing beneath for example) the construction costs do not normally allow for long gentle approaches. Nevertheless attempts should be made to avoid a slope of more than 1:15.
Width	Main routes: 1.8m (2 wheelchairs side by side) Secondary routes: 1.2m (1 wheelchair with pedestrian alongside)
Low edging rails/kerbs	Incorporate low rails or kerbs, at least 40mm high, along each side. These act as wheel stops for wheelchairs.
Surfaces	Where timber decking is used the timbers should be at right angles to the direction of travel and the gaps should be between 7-15mm. On ramped areas in particular give consideration to improving grip.
Passing places	If the bridge is narrow passing places may be desirable even on short lengths to allow for people resting to enjoy the view without interrupting the traffic. These should be of dimensions necessary to accommodate the typical users, e.g. wide enough for a wheelchair and one other person.
Handrails	Provide handrails or supports on both sides.
Approaches	Ensure a clear area of at least 1.5m length at both approaches. Use textured surfaces on approaches to provide warnings to visually disabled children.

4.10 Handrails

Handrails provide extra support for children with limited mobility, particularly alongside steps and slopes. Rails may also act as safety barriers, for example alongside paths which border open water or significant changes in ground level. The design and location of handrails must be appropriate to the stature and abilities of the children who are going to use them. It may not be possible to choose a rail height which suits all the children, especially if a school caters for a wide age range, in which case a double handrail may be the answer. Handrails must be securely anchored so that they withstand the weight of children leaning or pulling on them. Regular checks are important to ensure they remain safe. Variations in handrail texture and colour can be used to help differentiate areas for children with visual impairments.

	HANDRAIL DETAILS
Location	Provide handrails alongside steps, ramps and in locations where children with limited mobility are likely to need extra support. A rail on both sides will cater for children with the use of one arm. Handrails can also be used as protective barriers by open water, abrupt changes in level and other potentially hazardous areas.
Dimensions	Rail width: 45mm Rail height: This will depend on the age range of the children. Pay particular attention to semi ambulant children who rely heavily on a hand rail for support. Double rails will increase the range of heights catered for and may be necessary to serve both wheelchair users and semi-ambulant children. Rail length: Rails should extend approximately 500mm beyond the top and base of steps and ramps. Clearance of rail from adjacent wall: Minimum 45mm.
Design details	Select a rail which gives a comfortable grip; a round or oval section works well. Ensure that the ends of rails are rounded off or turned into the wall so that they do not create a hazard. Select handrails which contrast with the background so that they are easily discernible to children with visual impairments.
Materials	Take care to use materials which give a comfortable and firm grip. Metal can be unpleasant if cold or wet and is better coated with plastic or nylon. Hardwood is an attractive option but must be good quality to prevent splinters or cracks.

4.11 Gates

Gates provide a hybrid function in the landscape - they are entrance points which are also designed to act as barriers. Design and construction therefore requires an analysis of both the nature of the traffic that is intended to pass through, as well as that which it is intended to exclude. Children can usually be denied access simply by adding an extra catch which is too high for them to reach. The greatest challenges come when trying to prevent access by bicycles or motorbikes and yet still allow easy passage to wheelchairs. Solutions have been developed that rely upon an extended version of a 'kissing gate' which allows the wheelchair to be pushed into a recess adjacent to a swinging gate. In situations where full access is only required during periods when the grounds are supervised a much simpler solution may be the use of a simple locking gate or removable cross bars.

	GATE DETAILS
Width	Minimum clear opening of 900mm.
Opening	Handles for gates should be no higher than 750mm from the ground but may need to be much lower for some children. It may be desirable to fit handles at different heights. Self closing mechanisms have clear advantages but can make opening the gate more difficult for those with limited strength.
Design details	Ensure a clear area of at least 1.5m length on either side of the gate. Allow full room for access to the gate and also for waiting to one side if people are passing through. Use textured surfaces on approaches to provide warnings to visually impaired children.

Materials for paths and hard surfaces

	Main paths	Minor paths	Wheel-chair use	Semi-ambulant use	All-weather play	Fine-weather play	Cost
In-situ concrete	✔	✔	✔	✔	✔	✔	*

This is one of the cheapest options. It has a reputation for being unattractive, mainly due to uninspired design and construction, and it can give a high-glare finish (difficult for some types of visual impairment) and slippery surface. Even so, there are simple ways to ensure a reasonable finish. For example different textures can be applied to the surface, aggregates can be included in the general mix or on the surface, or the concrete can be used in combination with other materials such as brick paviors.

	Main paths	Minor paths	Wheel-chair use	Semi-ambulant use	All-weather play	Fine-weather play	Cost
Tarmac and asphalt (plus aggregate dressing)	✔✔	✔✔	✔✔	✔✔	✔✔	✔✔	***

Functionally these materials are hard to beat; they are hard wearing, last a long time, require minimal maintenance and are relatively cheap. With careful design these surfaces can work well aesthetically but if allowed to dominate large areas they can create a monotonous, bleak appearance. They are also painful to fall on.

Ways of improving their appearance:

Apply a surface dressing (which is boundbinding, not loose). Several options are possible:

- Small aggregates mixed with binder (tar, bitumen or adhesives): the aggregates can be of almost any colour but this is usually dependent on local supply.
- Aggregates coated in clear resin: more expensive but the resin protects the surface from dirt and weathering. Various proprietary brands are available - be selective as some give a shiny, unattractive finish and some can be slippery.

Paint patterns, shapes, games and features relating to the formal curriculum.

Break up large expanses of tarmac with some planting, fences, walls, raised planters etc.

Imaginative shapes - curves can help make things look more interesting and overcome the formality of standard rectangular playgrounds. Two linked smaller areas of tarmac may give more choice and variety than one large area.

	Main paths	Minor paths	Wheel-chair use	Semi-ambulant use	All-weather play	Fine-weather play	Cost
Self-binding gravel (including hoggin)	✔	✔[1]	✔			✔	*

As the name suggests, these are small particled, graded gravels which pack together to form a firm surface. If well constructed, this is a low cost, highly attractive, functional alternative to the more 'formal' materials. Success is largely dependent on the ability of the gravel particles to pack together and it is vital to ensure that the material and construction method are suitable. Some materials sold as 'self-binding gravels' do not pack very well but form loose, uneven surfaces which are prone to erosion and rutting. Construction methods should ensure an adequate sub-base and sufficient compaction of the gravel in successive layers. Try to find good local examples of self-binding gravel paths and to use the same source and specification (making sure they are appropriate for your soil type).

[1] Poor construction, inferior materials and heavy use by wheelchairs or cycles are likely to result in rutting.

	Main paths	Minor paths	Wheel-chair use	Semi-ambulant use	All-weather play	Fine-weather play	Cost
Loose gravels			✔[2]				*

It is not a good idea to use loose gravel for main access routes as it is unsuitable for wheelchair users and for some semi-ambulant children. Its real value lies in creating attractive areas for visual effect. Even then, regular maintenance may be necessary.

[2] Loose gravel is difficult for semi-ambulant and wheelchair users.

| * | low cost (< £25/m²) | ** | medium cost (£25-£35/m²) | *** | high cost (>£50/m²) (1996 prices) |

Materials for paths and hard surfaces

	Main paths	Minor paths	Wheel-chair use	Semi-ambulant use	All-weather play	Fine-weather play	Cost
Paving	✔	✔	✔	✔	✔	✔	*

(Sometimes referred to as small-unit paving). When used to good effect, paving provides an attractive alternative to other hard surfaces and helps to create a more intimate scale. All paving must be carefully laid to ensure level, even-jointed surfaces. Note that some paving may need an annual cleaning to remove a slippery layer of algae/moss which may develop.

Precast concrete slabs is the cheapest, available in a wide range of colour, shape, size and surface texture. Some are unattractive and some are slippery, especially when wet. Try to avoid using standard, grey 600mm x 600mm pre-cast concrete slabs, especially over large areas, as these tend to look dull and institutional.

Stone paving is attractive but expensive. Some stone paving can be slippery and slabs with very irregular surfaces can be a problem for semi-ambulant children and wheelchair users.

Crazy paving is relatively cheap, especially if there is a source of remnants available. When well constructed it can give a functional, attractive surface, although it is probably best not to use it too extensively. It is difficult with this material to control evenness of the surface and the width of joints and poor construction can result in an uneven surface, liable to trip children up, and the look of a failed attempt at DIY. Don't use very small pieces as they will become loose and very prone to frost heave.

Brick paviors are deservedly popular as they provide attractive, durable surfaces appropriate for many different types of use. Paviors are available as either concrete or clay in a vast range of colours, textures and prices. Concrete paviors are generally cheaper than clay but clay paviors are often more attractive. Avoid paviors that are very smooth and which can be slippery, especially when wet.

	Main paths	Minor paths	Wheel-chair use	Semi-ambulant use	All-weather play	Fine-weather play	Cost
Stone setts and cobbles	✔	✔	✔				***

These are available in a wide range of colour and size. Cobbles are usually sold in mixed batches and specifying particular grades will add to the cost. They are not recommended for main access routes but have a real value in adding aesthetic and textural interest. Their high cost (and it is illegal to collect cobbles from a beach or river!) usually limits use to small areas. They can be used as strips or bands to divide up areas of concrete or brick paving, or to denote the entrance into a smaller bay. Appropriate construction techniques are important if these materials are to form accessible surfaces. Ensure that setts are laid evenly. Cobbles can be set low in a mortar base to give a less bumpy surface and to help prevent them working loose (which is when they can become excellent missiles)!

	Main paths	Minor paths	Wheel-chair use	Semi-ambulant use	All-weather play	Fine-weather play	Cost
Timber	✔	✔[3]	✔				**

Wood is popular for its attractive, natural appearance and ability to blend well with informal landscape areas. Disadvantages include a relatively short life, although new techniques of preservation and adequate maintenance make it reasonable now to expect a 30-40 year life, even for timber which is in direct contact with soil. A greater problem is the tendency of timber to become slippery, especially if in a shaded, damp area. Ways of overcoming this include applying a coat of hot bitumen topped with sharp sand or covering the surface with wire netting but there is a risk of destroying the visual effect for which the timber is chosen. Even with such surfaces, regular maintenance will be necessary.

[3] Wooden planks should be laid at right angles to the direction of travel to prevent risk of wheels getting stuck in the grooves.

	Main paths	Minor paths	Wheel-chair use	Semi-ambulant use	All-weather play	Fine-weather play	Cost
Bark and wood chip			✔[4]	✔		✔	*

These are not generally recommended for main access routes unless the specification ensures that the paths will be sufficiently firm and durable to withstand frequent use.

[4] Deep layers of chips are too soft for wheelchair travel and tend to get boggy in the winter. It will only be appropriate for wheelchairs and cycles if a thin layer is laid over a firm but well-drained sub-base. Regular replacement or topping up will be necessary.

*	low cost (< £25/m^2)	**	medium cost (£25-£35/m^2)	***	high cost (>£50/m^2) (1996 prices)

4.12   Sources of information

References

Design Note 18: Access for disabled people to educational buildings, Department of Education & Science, 1984, HMSO, London.

Access design sheets, S.Thorpe, undated, Centre for Accessible Environments, London.

Informal countryside recreation for disabled people. Advisory Series No. 15, 1982, Countryside Commission, Cheltenham.

Beazley's design and detail of the space between buildings, A.Pinder & A.Pinder, 1990, E & FN Spon, London.

Mobility for special needs, Juliet Stone, 1995, Cassell, London.

Designing for the disabled, S. Goldsmith, 1976, RIBA Publications, London.

The wheelchair child, Philippa Russell, 1978, Human Horizons Series. Souvenir Press Ltd., London.

Organisations

British Standards Institution (BSI), 389 Chiswick High Road London W4 4AL 0171 629 9000

Access Committee for England, Unit 12, City Forum, 250 City Road, London EC1V 8AK 0171 250 0008

Centre for Accessible Environments (CAE), Nutmeg House, 60 Gainsford Street London SE1 2NY. 0171 357 8182

Mary Marlborough Centre, Nuffield Orthopaedic Centre, NHS Trust, Windmill Road, Oxford OX3 7LD 01865 227691.

Royal Association for Disability and Rehabilitation (RADAR), Unit 2, 250 City Road, London EC1V 8AF 0171 250 3222

RNIB/GDBA, Joint Mobility Unit, 224 Great Portland Street, London W1N 6AA, 0171 387 2233.

The Fieldfare Trust, 67a The Wicker, Sheffield, S3 8HT, 01742 701668.

The Sensory Trust, Swindon Environment Centre, 47b Fleet Street, Swindon SN1 1RE, 01793 526244.

Advice on accessible play facilities may be obtained from the organisations listed at the end of chapter 9.

Advice on specific special needs may be obtained from the organisations listed in chapter 15.

DESIGNING FOR SHADE, SHELTER AND SCREENING

5

5.1 Introduction

Designing school grounds as comfortable and secure environments relies a great deal on modifying the site's climate and character by providing shelter, shade and screening. Like many institutional landscapes, school grounds are often open expanses of land that offer little protection from cold winds or strong sunlight. Shelter and shade are essential to ensure that the outdoors is usable for as much of the school year as possible, especially for children who are frail or who are more sensitive to the extremes of temperature and sunlight. One characteristic of the UK climate is that it can change very suddenly from cool cloudy weather to scorching sunshine and flexible options are therefore needed.

5.2 Shade

Constant reminders from the medical profession have resulted in greater awareness of the dangers of exposing children's skin to strong sunlight. In many special schools there are often additional reasons for concern, for example some medications and medical conditions can result in skin reactions to sunlight. Children who are not independently mobile, and might spend prolonged periods in a wheelchair, are also of special concern. Shade is therefore a key issue.

Many school grounds have very little provision for shade. It may not be feasible in the short term to introduce shade into all the outdoor areas where it is needed and it is therefore important to identify priority areas. Of particular importance are places where children are likely to spend prolonged periods of time, such as playgrounds, sitting areas and outdoor classrooms. Dappled shade is generally more comfortable that dense shade and it is a good idea to plan for both short term and long term solutions.

Light conditions can be very important for children with visual impairments and can determine how much a child is able to see. Low light conditions can make it harder for many such children to identify contrasts. It is hard to generalise about requirements as they vary considerably with different types of visual impairment - some children find it easier to see under low light but many others need high light levels. Individual needs must therefore be taken into account.

Willow is a flexible material, here providing a shady tunnel.

There are various ways of providing shade:

Trees

Trees have the advantage of providing a visual and educational resource as well as a means of giving shade. They obviously do not provide an immediate solution as it takes time for them to mature but it is a good idea to plant trees for the long term. Choose trees with light or medium foliage to provide dappled shade (see 10.3), taking care to avoid ones with poisonous fruits or mucilaginous leaves (see 10.5). The shaded area will move with the sun so give careful thought as to the most appropriate places to plant them.

Portable furniture

Furniture, such as parasols and temporary canopies, have the advantage of providing immediate shade and can be moved to where they are needed. They can also be useful for occasional special events such as family picnics, fetes and open days. Large ones will shade areas sufficient for groups of children. The main disadvantage is that they will need storage room and they will need dismantling and setting up. These structures will require suitable base supports. Sometimes free-standing supports can get in the way, and may be hazardous for children with poor mobility or impaired sight, in which case it may be advisable to bury tubular supports in the ground (like the sockets for rotary clothes driers) so that the furniture can simply be plugged in when it is wanted.

Canopies attached to the building

These have a real value in creating outdoor areas which act as extensions to the building. These areas are within easy reach and have the added protection of the building. Canopies can be permanent but more flexibility is offered by ones which can be drawn out and put away as required. Make sure they extend out far enough to create a useful area of shade.

Landscape structures

Pergolas and trellis are attractive ways of providing dappled shade. Ensure that structures are sufficiently robust, well constructed and made of materials that will give a reasonable life span (brick, stone, metal or preserved timber). Also make sure that the support posts are positioned away from access routes so that they do not act as obstacles. Climbing plants can help to add to the shade and can grow very rapidly. However plant choice is important. Include climbers that will give a fairly even cover rather than relying on ones, like Clematis and honeysuckle, that make a 'bird nest' in one place. Avoid plants with poisonous berries or leaves (see 10.5). Make sure that there is sufficient distance between posts to allow for wheelchair movement.

A perogola covered in climbers can provide an effective shade.

5.3 Shelter

On exposed sites, and in parts of the country more prone to prevailing winds, shelter will be critical in extending use of the school grounds through a greater part of the year and to a greater range of special needs. Shelter from rain is also a sensible precaution in Britain. In order to plan effective shelter it is important to become familiar with the microclimate of the school as wind patterns will be influenced by existing tree and shrub plantings and by the building. A useful exercise is to monitor wind patterns throughout the site, noting wind tunnels and turbulence, sheltered areas and wind directions. Wind patterns may also change through the year so periodic monitoring is important.

There are various ways of creating shelter. Generally vegetation or structures that diffuse the wind are more effective than solid barriers. Complete shelter from rain obviously requires a solid overhead cover but semi-permeable canopies, such as mature trees, can be sufficient for brief showers.

Methods of providing shelter include:

Shelterbelts

Where space permits it is a good idea to plan shelter belts around the school perimeter. These also provide useful feeding and nesting sites for wildlife. Shelterbelts should be semi-permeable so as to filter the wind - solid masses of vegetation tend to deflect the wind and result in turbulence on their leeward side. These can be tree belts or tree and shrub belts and can include a mixture of evergreen and deciduous species. Appropriate species will be fast growing, tolerant of exposure and suitable for the particular site conditions. Refer to texts that outline suitable combinations of species (see last page of chapter) or contact local wildlife trusts or farm or countryside advisers for information (see chapter 15 for addresses of national organisations).

Hedges and structure planting

Shrub plantings can be used to provide more localised shelter within the school grounds, for example around a sitting area or outdoor classroom. Again, these should be semi-permeable to filter the wind. Informal hedges can include plants that will be useful for other purposes, for example as food plants for wildlife or to provide foliage, flowers or berries for classroom work or for craft activities.

Trellis with climbers

This is a way of providing localised shelter, perhaps for a sitting area. Include climbers that will give a fairly even cover over the trellis.

Trellis used to divide different spaces and to give shelter.

Walls and fencing

These can be very effective ways of providing localised shelter although careful design is important to reduce the risk of turbulence over the top and around the edges of solid structures. Climbing plants or wall plantings help prevent this and add interest.

Topography

Sometimes there is the option to sculpt the land so that more sheltered hollows are protected by surrounding mounds and planting. This sort of operation lends itself to the creation of an outdoor amphitheatre, for example. Take care to maintain good access to the lower level on the leeward side and make sure that surface water can drain away.

Extensions to the building

Semi-outdoor spaces created as extensions of the school building can take advantage of the shelter offered by the building itself. These structures include porches, covered walkways and terraces and fences or walls which extend as 'wings' from the building wall. These also have the advantage of giving shelter from rain.

Moveable shelters

These offer the advantage that they can be moved to different locations as needed. They can also be used to divide larger spaces into smaller ones or as the background for outdoor plays etc. Structures include curtains (net, cloth etc) hung on frames which are sturdy enough to remain stable but light enough to be moved around. More ambitious options include planted screens. Canopies hung over pergolas or frames will provide protection from rain.

5.4   Screening

It can be a challenge to screen unsightly or distracting views of outside elements such as traffic and unattractive buildings whilst retaining interesting views of cityscapes or countryside. Trees and shrubs can be used to screen views, bearing in mind that trees with clean trunks will only screen elevated views and that deciduous species will not provide screening in the winter. Careful 'layering' and grouping of planting from foreground to background and a strong foreground element (a special tree or sculpture) can be effective ways of both screening and highlighting views and can also create visual and spatial interest.

Noise and air pollution can be a nuisance for some schools, especially those with pupils who are easily distracted. Extremes (such as having a fire station next door) are hard to deal with but are often tolerable as long as they are relatively infrequent. Continuous noise such as that from heavy traffic can be much more disruptive. When considering remedial measures, it is important to recognise that research has shown that plants do little to reduce actual noise levels. They do often have a psychological value as people tend to think the noise is less intrusive if they can't see its source but this is of questionable application for children with limited or impaired perception skills. Soil is effective at reducing noise and earth mounds or willow walls are well worth considering.

Inside the building plants can help to 'absorb' noise although this effect is unlikely to be noticed in a carpeted room with a lot of soft furnishings. This can be helpful to children with impaired hearing who find it difficult to distinguish voices against background sounds. Plants can also help reduce levels of air pollution and this may be a consideration for children with asthma and other respiratory problems.

5.5   Sources of information

References

Beazley's design and detail of the space between buildings, A.Pinder & A.Pinder, 1990, E & FN Spon, London.

Informal countryside recreation for disabled people. Advisory Series No. 15, 1982, Countryside Commission, Cheltenham.

Hedging, 1988, British Trust for Conservation Volunteers, Oxon.

Landscape design in public open space, Nick Rowson & Peter Thoday, 1985, University of Bath.

The outdoor classroom, Building Bulletin 71, HMSO, London.

Woodlands, 1988, British Trust for Conservation Volunteers, Oxon.

Organisations

British Trust for Conservation Volunteers, 36 St. Mary's Street, Wallingford, Oxon OX10 0EU. 01491 39766

Countryside Commission, John Dower House, Crescent Place, Cheltenham, Glos GL50 3RA. 01242 52138

Farming and Wildlife Advisory Group, National Agricultural Centre, Stoneleigh, Kenilworth, Warwickshire CV8 2RX 01203 696699

DESIGNING FOR SOCIAL USE **6**

6.1　Introduction

The development of social skills is often a key theme in special education and this is generally a cross-curricular issue, drawing on many different facilities and settings. School grounds are generally geared more to physical activities, particularly playground games and sport, than to providing opportunities for children to engage in a wide range of social and passive uses. In the questionnaire used in LTL's research, many teachers commented on the lack of quiet areas, seating and choice of spaces in their school grounds and saw these as priority areas in future plans.

The design of the grounds, and the features within it, will determine the opportunities available to children and will influence patterns of behaviour and use. A range of spaces, of different styles and sizes, will help cater for different abilities, preferences and ages. A useful exercise, involving the children, is to identify activities that are wanted in the school grounds and to consider what types of spaces, furniture and fixtures are required. The following ideas might help:

Places to sit

- Lounging on the grass or on mats, bean bags, wedges.
- Private spaces and quiet areas.
- 'Secret' places or dens; woodland clearings, log piles, under trees and shrubs (with careful design these can give children a sense of privacy but still be within view of staff).
- Settings and themes for story telling.
- Views of active space, for example adjacent to play and sport areas.
- Eating and drinking; tables and chairs, picnic tables, litter bins, toilets.
- Views of water, wildlife and domestic animals.

Social events

- Barbecues and picnics.
- Fetes, festivals, marquee events.
- Open-air theatre, art displays.
- Plant sales, open days.

Outdoor recreation

- Camping; music; gardening; games.

Such uses of the grounds are generally less structured and some instances (e.g. chatting with friends) rely on some privacy and freedom from staff. This can be harder with children who require high supervision but sometimes the provision of a self-contained, safe area can give both pupils and staff more freedom. The same principle can also help children who need a chance to vent their frustrations - tantrums and aggressions can be safer outdoors.

Having identified potential uses, it is important to decide how a particular space will function. For example,

- Who is likely to use the space? Age group, ability range, group and/or individual, staff.
- When will it be used? Seasons, day and/or evening.
- What range of uses will it serve? Mainly passive or active use, curriculum areas, social uses.
- Will it be a self-contained area or will it link with other spaces?
- Does it need boundaries to prevent access out (or in) at certain times?
- What maintenance will be required?

6.2　Outdoor furniture

Seats

It is extraordinary that such a fundamental feature in the landscape has been so neglected in the design of special and mainstream schools. Consequently many schools have limited and inappropriate seating provision.

Bamboo providing shelter and enclosure for this seat.

There are two basic issues to keep in mind when planning seating; location and furniture design.

Location is extremely important; most children will be reluctant to sit in places where they feel isolated (away from activities and other children) or uncomfortable (exposed to winds or strong sun). Shelter and shade are very important, especially for children who are not very mobile and who are likely to get cold or sunburnt. Access to seats is also important and will be easiest if they are located on hard surfaces. Grass surfaces below seats, however attractive, are often inappropriate as with regular use of the seat the surrounds degenerate into a mud patch. Grouping seats is also important if you want to encourage social interaction. U or V shaped arrangements are better than a straight line.

The design of seats should ensure that they are comfortable and that they promote good posture. Children change size and proportion rapidly as they age and also different types of physical disability will call for particular design requirements so it is impossible to make specific recommendations in a general text. In many cases it will be necessary to ask the advice of a physiotherapist. As a general rule, seats with backs and arm rests are most appropriate for children who require physical support. Some types of bench include arm rests for each section of the seat and some incorporate a wide arm rest in the centre which provides a table top for books and drinks.

Seat dimensions need to relate to a child's stature and age. For some children a custom-made chair will be required while others will be able to make use of a wider range of furniture. Your school's indoor furniture will give you an idea of what dimensions and designs work best for different children and it can be good to get children involved in measuring each other and working out ranges of heights and how these relate to seat dimensions (by trying out seats with different heights and depths).

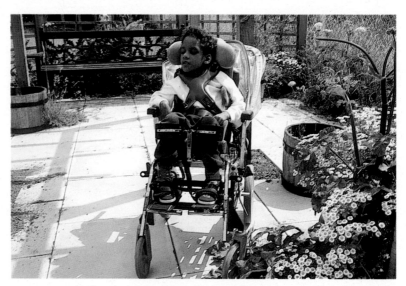

A sensory garden for wheelchair users to sit alongside others.

When selecting proprietary furniture take care to explain fully your school's requirements as few companies will be fully familiar with the needs of disabled children. There are companies who specialise in furniture for disabled people but take care to find out what types of disability they are designed for. Having seats custom made will enable you to specify exact requirements and to choose styles that fit in with the areas of the grounds where they are to be used. Some colleges design equipment and furniture for special needs and there are regional REMAP centres where volunteer engineers design equipment, mobility aids and furniture.

At times seats are likely to be used as supports by children with limited mobility and as play structures by the more active. Therefore, choose furniture that is robust and stable. With all furniture ensure that the design does not include small gaps where fingers can get caught and with wooden furniture ensure that they remain free of splinters. If there is a risk of furniture being stolen, or if children are likely to throw chairs around, it may be sensible to fasten furniture to the ground (using bolts or duck-bill anchors). Portable seats offer the advantage that they can be moved around as and when needed but some types are lightweight, not very stable and easily damaged.

Bean bags, large cushions, mats, tyres, hammocks, logs, stones and walls extend the range of seating options but may not be accessible to all children. It is important to allow sufficient space around seating for those who will remain seated in wheelchairs. Some schools for children with emotional and behavioural difficulties, have found that such items as bean bags are quickly wrecked by children and chairs and tables frequently damaged but that logs or railway sleepers are good as they are difficult to destroy. In such situations it can be useful to have access to a work-shop where furniture can be mended.

Tables are useful for outdoor classroom activities.

Tables

Tables are useful in the school grounds; they can serve as work areas, surfaces for food and drink, places to play cards and other table top games or simply as a focus for a group of children to sit round and chat. Take into account appropriate table heights - it will usually be necessary to include a range of heights but as a general rule they should be at least 720mm to ensure that wheelchair arms can fit underneath. Providing adequate clearance between table legs (or recessed legs) is important for wheelchair users. Children who use callipers and stand to work at a table require a different design. Tables with semi-circular cut-aways around the edge give children fuller access and these can be bought or made. Table surfaces should be carefully considered - avoid high glare surfaces as they can cause problems for children with visual impairments and can make it impossible for them to distinguish objects on the table. As with chairs, tables are likely to be leant against and stood on and should therefore be robust and stable.

Picnic tables are a good way of combining tables and chairs but the standard integrated design presents major access problems for children with physical disabilities. There are designs that are more suitable, for example ones which leave wheelchair space or which fix seats and table in a way that allows children access without having to climb over supports. The stability of tables is very important and they may need to be permanently anchored to the ground.

6.3   Eating outdoors

A bonfire site - accessible and safely away from the building.

Ensure that there is enough space and furniture for children to have drinks or lunch outside when the weather is good. Chairs, tables and litter bins will be needed, shade and shelter are also important (see chapter 5).

Picnics and barbecues can provide a focus for social events, in which case there must be sufficient space with an appropriate surface to accommodate a larger group. Barbecues are particularly suited to evening events and lighting will therefore need to be included in the area. With supervision, it may be appropriate for some children to have a chance to prepare and cook food. If so, barbecues must be at an appropriate height (adjustable ones will accommodate different statures and those working from a standing or seated position). Also, ensure there is adequate work surface to put utensils and food and that there is sufficient manoeuvring space around the barbecue. As a general safety precaution it is sensible to ensure that any circulation routes are away from the fire. For children with limited mobility or erratic movements a built-in barbecue will be safer than a portable type.

6.4   Outdoor events

Most schools organise occasional events in their school grounds, such as fetes, festivals, open days and performances. Many of these will require a large outdoor area. Such a space will be more interesting if it is sufficiently spread out, with shaded and open parts, to allow people to choose areas for sitting or walking. Grass areas should be well-drained and close-mown to maximise access for semi-ambulant children and wheelchair users. Path layouts (see chapter 4) and water points should take into account the location of such a gathering ground. Within this area there should be space for a marquee and, if power is required, it may be worth installing an outdoor electrical supply point. This will save running temporary cables each time which can be a hazard for semi-ambulant children and those with impaired vision.

If amphitheatres are planned, consider wheelchair access by designing paths sufficiently wide, ramps of appropriate gradient and incorporating hard surfaced seating spaces.

6.5   Social activities

Storytelling

Using different settings in the grounds (woodland, meadow, waterside etc) can help add atmosphere to different stories. This can also help encourage pupils to take an active part, perhaps by acting out different characters or creating stories for different locations.

Outdoor events

There are numerous options including outdoor performances, exhibitions of art, fetes, festivals and open days, all of which can involve families, the local community and other schools.

Newsletters, leaflets

These are a good way of spreading information about school grounds developments and activities and can involve children in a wide range of activities from planning, preparation of text and pictures and distribution.

Outdoor art

The outdoors provides all sorts of opportunities for art work; children can paint murals, create mosaics, make sculptures, collect natural materials (leaves, flowers etc) and make pictures and cards, draw and paint pictures of outdoor scenery and objects and make ceramic works and fire them in an outdoor kiln. Artists in residence is an excellent way of receiving input from an artist or sculptor and can result in all sorts of exciting grounds developments which involve the children.

Making table decorations

This is a good activity to tie in with an event such as a summer party or festive meal. Children can collect cut foliage and flowers from the grounds. These can be used to make a whole range of decorations, from placing in a bowl of water alongside floating candles to dry arrangements in Oasis. Some species, such as borage flowers, can be floated in cold drinks or frozen in ice cubes. Plants can also be a source of inspiration for decorative patterns on table covers or napkins.

Planning a picnic day

This can be a useful way of giving children the chance to meet different people and to take some responsibility for putting together an event. The lack of formality associated with a picnic, and the use of cold food, will remove some of the more stressful sides of food preparation and will mean there are less worries about spills and breakages. Activities can include planning and preparing invitations, calculating quantities and costs of food, visiting shops to buy food and preparing and arranging an outdoor area for use. Linked activities could include matching symbols and words to pictures of different foods; using vegetables and fruits grown in the grounds; studying the nutritional content or origins of different foods and designing/constructing picnic tables.

Running a theme day

Why not have a day when pupils and staff are encouraged to act out or participate in a particular theme? Many schools organise activities around national themes such as Apple Day, School Grounds Day and Tree Dressing Week but additional themes could include animals, explorers, science fiction, mystery (to solve), treasure hunt etc. It will be necessary to explain the activity to the children, ensuring they understand the overall theme and perhaps asking them to bring to school appropriate props such as clothes. A clear sequence of activities will need to be organised for the day and careful planning of how children are to participate. Linked activities could include writing about the day before and after it has happened, growing plants that can be used e.g. apples, halloween vegetables and making props for scenery, clothes and activities.

6.6   Sources of information

References

Informal countryside recreation for disabled people. Countryside Commission, 1994, Cheltenham.

Barrier free exterior design, Gary. Robinette, 1985, Van Nostrand Reinhold, New York.

Organisations

Countryside Commission, John Dower House, Crescent Place, Cheltenham, Glos GL50 3RA. 01242 521381

Nicholas Meech Environmental Art and Design, Little Bowley, Cadbury, Exeter, Devon EX5 5LA. 01884 855505 (Design and manufacture of countryside furniture).

Rehabilitation Engineering Movement (REMAP), National Organiser, Hazeldene, Ightham, Kent TN15 9AD. 01732 883818

Royal Association for Disability and Rehabilitation, (RADAR) Unit 2, 250 City Road, London EC1V 8AF 0171 250 3222

SENSORY EXPERIENCE

7

7.1   Introduction

It is widely accepted that children learn more effectively through a multi-sensory environment and there is increasing recognition of the potential value of school grounds for providing many different sensory experiences. Of course, stimulating senses is not an end in itself, but it can teach such skills as investigation, problem solving, anticipation and social integration. When planning for high sensory interest it is important to decide exactly what you want. There are three basic options:

- A self-contained area that concentrates a wide range of sensory experiences (often referred to as a 'sensory garden'. This is popular in special schools and many have developed, or are planning to develop, a sensory garden in their grounds. If designed well, such an area provides a valuable resource for the formal curriculum as the teacher will be confident of finding a wealth of educational material available. You need to decide whether or not children will be allowed access to the area, either independently or under supervision, during break times as this will require greater emphasis on features associated with recreation.

- A sensory trail or route that includes a variety of experiences. The trail has similar objectives to the sensory garden in providing a range of experiences for children but it has more association with movement. It can therefore have a direct application to teaching orientation skills. For example as children with visual impairments become more familiar with the trail, they learn to recognise different sounds, textures and smells along the trail and gain confidence in their own abilities to interpret the environment and find their own way. It can also help develop physical mobility skills in children; some may be encouraged to travel further, and therefore to extend their capabilities, and some may learn to deal with surfaces they are not accustomed to or to walk in a straight line (something that children with sensory impairments often have problems with).

- Enriching all (or most) areas of the school grounds. School grounds that are relatively diverse and easily accessible may lend themselves to developing an overall theme of sensory interest rather than concentrating on specific areas. It can also be argued that even schools that develop sensory gardens or trails should have an overall aim of high interest throughout their grounds, even if this takes many years to achieve.

All landscapes induce sensory responses but it is the concentration of different experiences that gives sensory gardens and trails their identity. Most are passive places, designed to be inviting and comfortable. Some are designed to stimulate children while others are aimed more at restful effects, particularly useful for helping to calm hyperactive and easily distracted children.

They are also places where the normal rules of behaviour may be deliberately relaxed as children are encouraged to explore, touch, pick and crush plants or interact with objects. This places certain challenges on the design, particularly a need to make things fairly robust and to choose plants that can tolerate the inevitable damage from a lot of inquisitive hands. It also calls for careful interpretation; children need to be aware of what is permissible behaviour.

In order to maximise the value of certain experiences unusual design approaches may be required. For example, trees may be deliberately planted near to a path so that the bark can be felt rather than setting it back as it would be an ordinary design. Children must be able to get around the area but it may be interesting to include path surfaces whose textures give different and more challenging experiences of a type that would not be encountered on main access paths. An extension of this idea would be the provision of slopes or other features to test or stretch mobility skills.

The areas also call for different management techniques. For example there may be a deliberate policy to retain lower tree branches to enable children to balance and climb on them and to prune shrubs and trees into interesting shapes.

Historically many sensory gardens were focused on people with visual impairments. Sadly, many designers made the mistake of assuming that, because a child has a reduced sensory range, they need an over-emphasis of the remaining senses. Thus many early sensory gardens focused on too few sensory experiences (failing to appreciate that children with visual impairments often have some residual sight) and were simply collections of scented plants. In practice of course many visually impaired people have heightened awareness of other senses and can easily be overpowered by crude stimuli en masse. The principle holds true for many other forms of sensory impairment.

Successful design is largely based on imaginative approaches and finding ways of concentrating or 'stage managing' events (such as dovecotes so that birds can be seen) and experiences (such as splashing water, playing with autumn leaves) that would normally require venturing further afield. It is an ideal project in which to involve an artist or sculptor who can provide stimulating settings for all-season sensory experiences.

7.2   Ideas and inspiration

It is worth remembering that there are many sensations we experience that are not formally categorised as one of the five senses, for example gravity, temperature, change, space and enclosure. The following lists are intended to offer some ideas which highlight the many different sensory experiences.

Looking, seeing

COLOUR: Plants offer a complete spectrum of colour with the added delight of changes throughout the different seasons. Include flowers, leaves, bark, berries, lichens and mosses. As well as providing a range of colour experiences, if space permits, single colour themed areas can be considered that can be used to explore moods and atmosphere. Hard materials can provide a richness of colours and textures (stone, old brick, gravel, slate) or simple materials can be used to create patterns of colour (mosaics, murals, paving). Also consider changes in appearance and colour of materials when wet and dry (pebbles in water).

An imaginative use of materials combining interesting colour, texture and patterns.

SHAPE: Most objects can be used although many natural materials are quite complex shapes. For simple, distinctive shapes consider; leaves (sycamore, beech, ash), fruits (apples, currants, rose hips), flowers (daisy, poppy, bell flowers), stems (bamboo canes, dead nettle - square stems), paving (hexagons, squares, triangles) and plant containers (round, square, rectangular).

MOVEMENT: Good for stimulating interest and for improving attention spans, especially if movement is combined with sound. Consider; trees (aspen, willow, white poplar), grasses, mobiles, chimes, animals, water, moving sculptures. Locate some within reach so that children can activate them. Place wind-activated items in places likely to receive some breeze.

CONTRAST: Children with visual impairments who have some residual sight may be able to distinguish contrasting materials. Consider; hard surfaces and markings, kerbs and edgings, flowers, foliage, sculptures.

PATTERNS: These are important in helping children learn to identify different objects and can also inspire art work. Regular patterns are provided by; brick work, paving, cobbles, fencing, dandelion clocks and pine cones and more random patterns by; bark (plane, birch, eucalyptus), variegated leaves, skeleton leaves.

Murals are an excellent way of enlivening buildings and adding sensory interest.

Everyday objects (bicycle parts) built into a sensory design.

Hard materials can provide fascinating patterns.

Listening, hearing

Children often need to be encouraged to listen to sounds, especially to more subtle ones. Organisers of nature studies often find listening activities to be a good way of calming children and tuning them in to their

environment. Consider both sounds that occur naturally and those that can be activated by the children. Natural sounds include; leaves rustling in the wind, birds singing, water tricking / dripping / splashing, rain on an overhead cover. Activated sounds include; splashing water, striking chimes and sound sculptures. Deaf children will be able to sense vibrations and percussive sounds and these can be provided through sculpture and features such as deer-scarers (chinese tapping water features). "Sound fences", activated by dragging a stick along a series of lengths of tubing or piping are melodious and fun.

Feeling, touching

The outdoors is full of different textures and children with visual impairments in particular rely on these to interpret the environment. Options include; rough surfaces (lichens, stone wall, bark); smooth (pebble, polished wood, leaves, flower petals); ridged (textured concrete, backs of leaves); hairy (animals, leaves such as Stachys, buds, grass); bumpy (cobbles, twigs). Also think of objects that illustrate simple shapes (circular flowers, cubic containers, oval fruits,

A captivating feature; moving water splashes onto mirrored glass.

triangular ivy leaves etc); weight (light bark, heavy clay etc); temperature (sun-warmed water, cold shaded water; stone next to soil); wet and dry (moist and dry soil/sand, freshly shed leaves and older dry ones); contrasting densities (hard stone and soft moss). Many non-disabled children underestimate the value of texture when deciphering their environment and they can learn a great deal from studying alongside visually impaired children.

Smelling

Although most attention has been given to scented plants there are many other materials that have distinctive and interesting smells. With plants, consider different types of scent: scents that fill the air and can be smelt without touching the plant (Mock orange (Philadelphus), some roses, winter honeysuckle, curry plant, cut grass, hay); Intimate scents where the flowers need to be investigated (violet, primrose, some Narcissus); Activated scents which are released when plant parts are crushed (most culinary herbs, scented geranium). Another option is for children to try to identify the scents from different distinctive herbs, such as peppermint and apple mint, lemon thyme and curry plant. There can be interesting

A music garden inviting interaction.

differences between people's abilities to detect the more subtle scents, such as violets and primroses, and it can be a fun exercise to get children to run a survey of the class. Some plant scents can be a problem for

Open air music - instruments built into the trees.

Orientation, gravity and balance

Aspects of path design, such as width, change in direction, branching, slopes and ability to see a destination or end point all influence speed of travel and sense of mystery and invitation. Therefore paths in sensory gardens and trails can be seen to have much more potential than simply providing direct access. Orientation skills may also be developed by providing things for children to stand on or climb up (logs, trees, platforms, bridges, stages) that test or develop balance and which act as markers in the landscape. For some children the teaching objective may be to introduce such basic concepts as up, down, high and low (this may be done by incorporating objects that can be repositioned such as hanging baskets and mobiles).

children with asthma, particularly the more powerful scents and those coupled with flowering and therefore pollen release. Other options include a whole range of familiar smells (pond water, wood shavings, autumn leaves, cut grass). The effects of water on smells can be interesting (wet soil, stone, leaves). Also consider ways of teaching children how smells can help people detect hazards, for example smoke from a fire.

Tasting

Taste can be a useful way of demonstrating where food comes from and showing children the link between growing and eating. However it is important to ensure that children remain cautious about unidentified plants and it is probably necessary to restrict the choice to those food plants which are clearly recognised, such as apples.

Enjoying the scent of a herb leaf.

Variety in path texture and colour provide for a range of experiences.

Cause and effect

Some children have problems understanding the concept of cause and effect. This can be demonstrated very effectively through a range of practical outdoor features such as interactive sculptures on which children can pull levers, press switches or activate touch-sensitive pads to produce

Textures built into the wall for young hands to explore.

Plastic balls run along a series of gulleys, a good way of illustrating movement and cause and effect.

The jungle tunnel invites exploration and reaction.

different effects. Other possibilities include gear wheels, pulleys, balances and water which moves through a series of pools or channels.

Moods

The design of quiet and relaxing areas may be a worthwhile consideration in schools where the children need a calming influence. Many schools have reported that such environments are useful for counselling. There may be value in creating other types of atmosphere, for example through the use of shade and light, enclosure and sounds to explore other moods.

7.3   Sources of information

References

Plants for play, Robin Moore, 1993, MIG Communications, Berkeley, California, USA.

Fun and games, Judy Denziloe, 1994, Butterworth Heinemann, Oxford.

The healing garden, 1993, Sue Minter, Headling Book Publishing Ltd., London.

Gardening without sight, Kathleen Fleet, 1989, RNIB, London.

Scented flora of the world, an encyclopaedia, R. Genders, 1978, Granada Publishing, Mayflower.

The garden and the handicapped child, Patricia Elliott, 1978, The Disabled Living Foundation, London.

Organisations

Centre for Environmental Interpretation, Metropolitan University of Manchester, Lower Chathm Steet. Manchester M15 6BY 0161 247 2000

Sensory Trust, White Barn Farmhouse, Swinden Environment Centre, 47b Fleet Street Swindon SN1 1RE 01793 526244

Royal National Institute for the Blind, 224 Great Portland St., London W1N 6AA. 0171 388 1266

Royal National Institute for the Deaf, 19-23 Featherstone Street London EC1Y 8SL 0171 296 8000

DESIGNING FOR PHYSICAL ACTIVITY

8

8.1 Introduction

Physical activity is fundamental to children's development; it helps them explore and experience their environment, interact with others, use gross and fine motor skills and give meaning to things around them. Lack of movement and exercise has serious implications for the physical, intellectual, personal and social development of all children, including (and perhaps particularly) children with special needs.

Children with special needs generally have limited opportunities to participate in many of the outdoor activities which other children take for granted. There is a tendency for children with special needs to lead relatively 'protected' home lives and the importance of them participating in a wide range of outdoor activities may not be realised. Many have limited chance to play with other children at home. Therefore it is especially important for schools to provide these experiences. With children who have had little experience of outdoor activity there may be a need to teach them how to participate.

Some children need regular physiotherapy and there can be opportunities for combining sessions with outdoor activities if appropriate facilities are available. Quiet areas can provide a setting for stretching and positioning exercises on soft mats, cushions and wedges while sports and play facilities can provide for physical skills requiring greater exertion.

8.2 Sport and organised games

Sports and organised games can help children to develop a wide range of physical skills, particularly balance, co-ordination, dexterity and stamina. Group sports teach the importance of cooperation, sharing, responsibility and turn taking whilst individual games (such as skipping and ball games) can be popular leisure activities. Hyperactive children are given something purposeful to channel their energies, inactive children are encouraged to move and children with sensory impairments gain confidence in mobility. All children can be helped to develop a better awareness of body image and movement, to learn more self-control and greater responsiveness.

Although some sports can share the same outdoor area, there is likely to be a need for a series of spaces catering for different types of activity. Try to integrate these spaces with the rest of the landscape by setting them into informally shaped areas with perimeter tree and shrub planting. The latter will also help create shelter and shade. With ball games, children with poor co-ordination are likely to find it hard to keep the ball within the defined area and a physical retainer, such as earth mounds around the perimeter, can help.

Many sports and games can be played by children with disabilities although some equipment and techniques may need to be modified. For example, it may be better to use a smaller court for sports such as badminton, a lighter ball for volley ball, cricket and rounders, lighter racquets and bats, shorter handled racquets, additional stabilisers for cycling and skiing, and adjustable heights of table tennis, darts boards and archery targets. Different techniques may include a simplified scoring system, allowing children to let the ball bounce twice before they hit it in games like tennis or to use underarm bowling in cricket. Children who are keen to participate in wheelchair athletics will need a sports wheelchair and an appropriate track. Some sports will be unsuitable for some children. For example, contact sports present a high risk of injury to children with haemophilia or with brittle bones. Careful judgement will need to be used if introducing children to sports using hard or heavy equipment which could be dangerous if misused.

8.3 Outdoor pursuits

Many types of outdoor pursuit are suitable for children with special needs, although some require adaptation of technique or equipment.

Camping can be done within the school site, if there is room. Tents with no central upright poles and sufficient space inside are better for children with limited mobility and wheelchair users. Proximity to toilets is important.

Fishing can be a school or local activity if there is access to a suitable river. Adaptations include platforms designed for wheelchair users, supports for fishing rods and lightweight equipment

Fitness trails include features to develop a range of skills.

Orienteering has proved to be a popular activity which can be adapted for a wide range of needs. Trails can be modified to a suitable length and challenge and maps can be produced in text, symbol or Braille form or as recorded messages, as appropriate.

Rock climbing is available at most activity centres. Climbing walls are an option in schools and are particularly suitable for an older age group.

Walking, rambling and hill walking provide can be provided for by schools with sizeable grounds. There are now many trails designed to be wheelchair accessible and with good interpretation for those with sensory impairments.

Water-based activities such as sailing, rowing and canoeing are provided in some schools but are mainly limited to activity centres. Adaptations include modified canoes and boats and stabilisers. Good instruction and safety are essential.

For many schools it will not be practical to try to provide for many of these in the grounds but activity centres throughout the country offer excellent opportunities for children to participate in a range of challenges (such as rock climbing and sailing) and to mix with other children. Day visits or longer stays are possible are most centres. Activities are offered for a range of skills and perseverance levels, and the settings in which they take place are varied.

8.4   Physical activities

Basic movements

There are many activities that can help develop children's body awareness and mobility skills. Examples include encouraging a child to follow the line of a rope laid on the ground, to walk backwards, to run across an open space (this can be good for children with visual impairments with limited confidence in moving), to cross a space on a series of logs and stones without touching the ground or to change direction in response to visual or acoustic cues.

Throwing a ball is a simple and effective way of developing skills in co-ordination and team work. Variations on a theme include seeing how far or how high a child can throw, throwing the ball in an arc, close to the ground, over an object or at a target. Variety can be introduced by using different sizes and weights of ball. It is best to do these activities within the sports area, particularly if it has got retaining nets to prevent the ball finishing up in unexpected places.

Large ball being used to encourage basic movements.

Setting up an obstacle course

An obstacle course is a good way of providing many different types of challenges. It can help develop physical skills, confidence, perseverance and self-control, encourage inactive children to move and give

Trim trails are particularly popular with very active children.

opportunities for children to succeed. The particular range of equipment and length of course will obviously depend on the ability range of the children. Materials might include (either already constructed or ready to be put together) logs and tree stumps, balancing beams, ladder, tyres and plastic hoops. A section of wide concrete pipe can serve as a tunnel but take care that exposed edges are made safe (e.g. by covering with rubber or timber) and that the pipe is sufficient short and wide to ensure that children cannot get stuck. Additional activities could include children planning the course, visiting a fitness training circuit to test different equipment and to see which would be most useful and drawing pictures and/or writing a description of each activity.

Activities requiring less exertion

Some children will not be able to participate in very active pursuits but less demanding activities may be suitable. Examples include Frisbee, mini golf, kite flying, croquet and fishing.

Wheelchair accessible fishing platform.

8.5   Sources of information

References

Give us the chance: sport and physical recreation with people with a mental handicap, Revised Edition, Kay Latto & Barbara Norrice, 1989, Disabled Living Foundation, London.

Informal countryside recreation for disabled people. Advisory Series No. 15, 1982, Countryside Commission, Cheltenham.

Out of doors with handicapped people, Mike Cotton, 1981, Souvenir Press.

Outdoor adventure for handicapped people, Mike Cotton, 1983, Souvenir Press.

Physical education for handicapped children, Sarah George and Brian Hart, 1983, Souvenir Press, London.

The outside classroom, Margot Walshe, 1993, Surrey County Council, Kingston-on-Thames.

Organisations

British Standards Institution (BSI), 389 Chiswick High Road, Chiswick N4 4AL. Tel: 0171 629 9000.

British Sports Association for the Disabled (BSAD), The Mary Glen Haig Suite, Solecast House, 13-27 Brunswick Place, London N1 6DX. Tel: 0171 490 4919.

The National Federation of Anglers, Halliday House, Egginton Junction, Derbyshire DE65 6GU. Tel: 01283 734735.

National Playing Fields Association (NPFA) 25 Ovington Square, London SW3 1LQ. Tel: 0171 584 6445.

Riding for the Disabled Association, Avenue R, National Agricultural Centre, Kenilworth, Warwickshire CV8 2LY. Tel: 01203 696510.

Sports Council, 16 Upper Woburn Place, London WC1H 0QP. Tel: 0171 388 1277.

DESIGNING FOR OUTDOOR PLAY

9.1   Introduction

The importance of play for the physical, emotional, intellectual and social development of children is well recognised in special education. Through different play activities children can learn motor skills (balance, co-ordination, dexterity etc); social skills (sharing, helping, communicating, etc); intellectual skills (numeracy, colours, shapes, vocabulary, etc); and creative skills (constructing, imagining, role-playing etc). For children with learning difficulties play can be a good way of reinforcing basic concepts such as up and down, fast and slow, light and heavy.

Playhouses are popular and can be brightened by murals.

The role of play for teaching social skills may also be particularly important. Some children do not know how to play and how to share, take turns or compete in a non-aggressive way. Competitive or team games can be particularly difficult. Play therapy is advocated as a means of teaching children these social skills and usually involves the use of basic materials such as sand or water to work through concepts such as cause and effect.

School grounds have the potential to provide a wealth of opportunities for children with special needs to play. The results of the LTL questionnaire showed that many schools consider their existing play provision to be limited and would like to develop further facilities to provide for a wide range of uses, ages and abilities.

Variety is particularly important to encourage children to explore and investigate and to develop self-expression and creativity. School grounds often lack any sense of mystery and large expanses of grass and tarmac leave little to the imagination.

Opportunities for both active and less physically demanding play are important. Quiet areas and play houses tend to be popular (especially with children who do not participate in the more active forms of play) and they provide for a type of social interaction not catered for in an open playground. Many schools also emphasise the importance of hands-on experience, particularly for children with learning difficulties, and creative

Grass mounds are popular for rolling, climbing and hiding.

activities are therefore valuable. Providing quiet areas adjacent to a playground will help avoid children feeling excluded. On the other hand, providing play opportunities that are too challenging or not challenging enough for children is likely to result in feelings of frustration, disinterest and boredom.

Some children with special needs associate play time with a time when they are bullied by other children. These problems have to be addressed as part of an overall school policy but the design of play areas has been shown to have a bearing. A focus on one large play area, usually dominated by ball games, gives children no chance to avoid confrontation or to find alternative play activities to participate in.

9.2 Spaces for play

There are some key requirements that need to be met by the design of school grounds. One is the wide variety of opportunities needed to satisfy the different types of play and different teaching aims. There is a tendency to focus attention on fixed play equipment and playgrounds but these will only cater for certain types of activity. The concept of providing opportunities for a wide range of outdoor play should be applied to as much of the school grounds as possible. For example, gentle grass mounds can easily be designed into the landscape as features for children to roll down, to run up and down or to hide behind. Just as important are informal

Play fences can include different features and are a good way of dividing up a play space.

areas with materials that can be used to construct things as part of creative and imaginative play (twigs, cones, stones, wood etc) and settings that encourage exploration.

Another challenge is to plan play opportunities that are safe and accessible but at the same time attractive to children; there is no point in providing expensive play materials if children are not inspired by them. Involving children in the planning process is one of the best ways of ensuring that the play area will provide the sorts of experiences they would like.

In planning the realisation of these ideas it is important to consider the following issues:

- Children's abilities and preferences.

- Not all play activities needs to be accessible to all of the children. Try to anticipate the likely usage patterns - are more boisterous children likely to knock into frailer children?

- In most schools there will be children who want to charge about and others who are happier quietly playing in a sand pit. Think about zoning play spaces into different zones, possibly for different ages or different abilities. In many cases if play facilities are well selected and provide a range of challenges the children may naturally segregate by activity and temperament.

A wide slide can be used by child and helper together.

Access

- Children must be able to get to the play area from the school building so don't just think about access within the play space itself. Consider connecting the play areas to main access paths and ensuring that gates are sufficiently wide for wheelchairs and can be opened easily (but can also be locked to prevent access).

- Within each play area there must be access to each play activity (and equipment) and to seats. See chapter 4 for advice on surfaces.

- Each play structure must have sufficient space around it (separate to main access routes) to enable children to climb on and off without risk of colliding with other children.

- Is there is sufficient space to cater for the required number of children?

- Will children want to use the play facilities?

- Does it look interesting and fun?

- Has it been designed to meet the children's identified needs?

- Is it well cared for?
- Are there opportunities for climbing, swinging, sliding, interactive play, creative play etc.
- Does it provide opportunities for the appropriate range of abilities and ages.

Types of use

- The best play facilities will cater for many different types of use and this will often involve a collection of different spaces. Consider opportunities for the following:
- Active use: walls to play ball games against, climbing wall, open space for kickabout, tag and running, playground markings for hopscotch and marbles, hard surfaced routes for wheeled toys and bikes, assault course or fitness circuit, play equipment and objects for climbing, swinging, jumping, balancing etc.
- Passive and social use: quiet areas for sitting, reading and chatting, tables for card games , tables and chairs for eating outside, weeping trees and shrubs for sitting under, socialising and playing games, attractive areas for walking, activities to watch.
- Creative use: walls and surfaces for art work, shrubs and trees for sculpting, materials for craft and art work, theme gardens for linked activities such as cooking or drying herbs, areas for staging art work, storytelling and outdoor plays, interactive sculptures.

Imaginative play equipment design.

'Wibbly-wobbly way' - accessible to all children.

Play equipment

There is a wide range of proprietary play equipment available but look carefully at what the different manufacturers offer. Few sales representatives will have more than a superficial awareness of the needs of children with special needs and none will be familiar with the particular needs of your pupils. So it is essential to provide as full a brief as possible and to involve the children in choosing different equipment and, if possible, trying out some. Make sure you are kept fully informed of the intentions of the designer We have seen examples of structures which sounded perfect at the planning stage but which have ended up, after construction, behind a padlocked gate because they were not safe to use.

9.3 Safety

Equipment

- Are there safety surfaces under all play equipment from which children could fall?
- Is there a clear route through the playground, is this sufficiently wide and is it sufficiently far from the pieces of play apparatus?
- Is there sufficient space around equipment to allow children to climb on and off and to manoeuvre and stand wheelchairs without risk of collisions from passing children?
- Does it conform to European safety standards?

Although not mandatory, it is recommended that the manufacture and installation of play equipment meets the standards outlined in British Standard 5696 (or in the German standards, DIN 7926) However, bear in mind that these standards do not address special needs and therefore provide only a baseline of safety as there are likely to be additional standards that relate to the specific needs of your pupils.

Self-built equipment must also be of high standard. It is good practice to have design details and final construction checked by the County Inspectorate or Health and Safety Officer to ensure that the equipment conforms to British safety standards.

Regular maintenance is essential to ensure that play resources remain safe. Ensure that equipment is routinely checked and that there is a system in place for recording, and acting on, any problems.

Safety surfacing

British Standard 5696 (1990) recommends that impact-absorbing surfacing is installed under and surrounding equipment from which there is a possibility of falls from a height over 600mm. Unfortunately, there is no single material that works best as a safety surface; all have advantages and disadvantages which need to be weighed up according to patterns of use and ability ranges of children.

MATERIALS FOR SAFETY SURFACING	
Loose-fill materials:	
Chipped bark or wood	Relatively cheap and easy to lay, gives good impact absorption (at correct depth), and provides an attractive surface.. It requires regular maintenance (cleaning, raking, topping up).
Sand	A relatively cheap material with good impact absorption. Can be kicked or thrown around. Litter and fouling by animals can be a problem. Regular maintenance is required (cleaning, raking and topping up). Unsuitable for wheelchairs and semi-ambulant.
Synthetic surfaces:	
(e.g. rubber tiles, shredded rubber, wet-pour rubber.)	Long-lived, low maintenance surface. Suitable for wheelchairs. Impact absorption varies with make and thickness. Expensive and more prone to vandalism.

9.4   Adventure play

Adventure play was developed in reaction to the general inadequacy of ordinary play areas to provide for more than a narrow range of activities. It is very popular in special schools and many have developed, or are planning to develop, areas for adventure play. Whilst many of the same principles outlined above apply, there are some specific issues concerning this type of provision.

The design of an adventure playground should aim to maximise opportunities for children to be creative, to explore and to use imaginative play. Informal settings, such as woodlands, lend themselves to this theme and mounds, slopes, banks and hollows can be incorporated to add variety. Trees are good for climbing, swinging from on ropes or hiding behind and can be characters in children's fantasy play. Shrubs can be hiding places or sources of materials for other things, such as willow wands for craft work. Loose materials such as twigs, leaves, cones, seed keys, soil and sand stimulate creative play. Wood, bricks, stones and sand can be used to build things. Sand is an excellent material; it is fun to touch and offers endless possibilities for being moulded, poured, mixed with water, transported etc. Piles of leaves are also popular and if the area does not naturally collect a lot of leaf litter it may be possible to collect it from other parts of the school grounds. These areas also benefit from the addition of portable play equipment and materials such as tyres, logs, wooden planks and bricks. These can be changed if the children grow tired of them. Fitness training circuits, obstacle courses and assault courses can be built into adventure areas depending on the particular abilities and ages of the children.

Obstacle trail made from low-cost, wooden structures.

Rope swing over deep bark.

Surfaces should be accessible and safety surfacing should be used under swings and equipment and areas for climbing. However, it will be important to select materials which are in keeping with a more informal setting. As children are actively encouraged to explore materials it is especially important to keep these areas free of litter (especially glass and metal) and poisonous plants and to ensure that equipment is regularly checked and maintained

> "*Play therapy techniques (such as sand and water play, building and knocking down) can begin to allow such children to learn how to share and co-operate, to learn social skills and to take pleasure and pride in what they are doing. By using the rough-and-ready materials available in a garden, such work can be undertaken without the adolescent perceiving it as 'babyish' or being mocked by his peers".*
>
> Caroline Reeves, Pitmore School.

9.5   Sources of information

References

Accessible play, Mary Januarius, 1995, ILAM/HAPA, Reading.

Let me play, Jeffrey, McConkey & Hewson, 1988, Souvenir Press, London.

Give us the chance: sport and physical recreation with people with a mental handicap, Revised Edition, Kay Latto & Barbara Norrice,1989, Disabled Living Foundation, London.

Innovation in play environments, Paul Wilkinson (ed), 1980, Croom Helm Ltd, London.

The outside classroom, Margot Walshe, 1993, Surrey County Council, Surrey.

Meldreth series games, Mike Ayres Designs, 1990, unit 8 Shepherd Grove, Stanton, Bury St. Edmunds, Suffolk, IP31 2AR Tel: 01359 251551 (video showing range of adapted games for children with physical disabilities)

Play and disability, Calum McLeod, 1995, National Centre for Play, Edinburgh.

Play therapy, an introductory paper, 1995, National Centre for Play, Edinburgh.

Organisations

British Standards Institution (BSI), 389 Chiswick High Road, London W4 4AL 0181 996 7111.

Handicapped Adventure Play Association (HAPA), Fulham Palace, Bishop's Avenue, London SW6 6EA. 0171 731 1435.

Play Leisure Advice Network (PLANET), Cambridge House, Cambridge Grove, London W6 0LE 0181 741 4054

Play and Disability Alliance (PADA), 6 Tavistock Road, Jesmond, Newcastle upon Tyne NE2 3JA. 0191 286 6687

National Play Information Centre (NPIC), 199 Knightsbridge, London Sw7 1DE 0171 584 6464

National Centre for Play (NCP), Moray House College of Education, Holyrood Road, Edinburgh EH8 8AQ. 0131 556 8655.

National Playing Fields Association (NPFA) 25 Ovington Square, London SW3 1LQ. 0171 584 6445.

USING PLANTS IN THE LANDSCAPE 10

10.1 Introduction

Plant material performs many different functions in the landscape. It is not within the scope of this publication to detail the general use of plants in school grounds but this chapter will highlight those issues which are particularly relevant to school grounds design for children with special needs. For more general information reference should be made to the sources of information listed at the end of the chapter.

The use of plants that serve more than one role in the landscape is particularly appropriate for school grounds which aim to create a multi-sensory environment with maximum opportunities for use. Although many plants will be chosen primarily to perform a particular role, such as shelter, many have useful secondary qualities. For example, shelter belts can include plants that also provide educational material, a food source or nesting site for wildlife, raw materials for craft work or a means of inspiring play. Plants whose parts can be harvested, taken inside and used in craft and art work may be particularly useful.

10.2 Structure planting

An important use of woody plants is to give a framework to the school grounds and effectively to divide the landscape into a series of different spaces. Institutional landscapes are characterised by a lack of structure planting which leaves them bare and exposed. Planting to provide shelter and shade can be especially important for those children who need greater protection from winds and direct sunlight.

Tree and shrub plantings can enhance the appearance of the school and define different spaces.

Plants to be used in this way should be hardy, robust and long-lived with minimal maintenance demand. Where shrub plantings are used to divide spaces it is worth considering children's scale. Plantings between 1m and 1.75m can give children the feeling of privacy but still allow adults a clear view. This also applies to mazes. It is advisable to avoid using prickly, abrasive and poisonous plants, especially where children are likely to use plants to hide in or to play near.

EXAMPLES OF STRUCTURE PLANTS:

Tall:	*Eleagnus ebbingei*, *Salix spp.* (willow), *Corylus avellana* (hazel), *Viburnum tinus*, *Kerria japonica*, Bamboos.
Low/medium:	*Viburnum tinus* 'Eve Price', *Hypericum* 'Hidcote', *Spiraea japonica*.
Plants for hedges:	*Crataegus monogyna* (hawthorn), *Fagus sylvatica* (beech), *Prunus cistena* 'Crimson Dwarf', *Cotoneaster lacteus* & *C. simonsii*, *Ilex aquifolium* (holly).

Weeping trees are good to hide under.

Children who use wheelchairs or other mobility aids often have fewer chances to play in and among plants, usually because there is no access. Incorporating trees and shrubs with weeping branches planted into an accessible surface (such as self-binding gravel) can offer these experiences to such children.

10.3 Trees

Trees can provide both shelter and shade. However, heavy shadows can be oppressive and can be avoided by choosing light-foliaged trees that give dappled shade such as *Gleditsia triacanthos* and *Sorbus aucuparia*. Late leafing trees, such as *Robinia pseudoacacia* and *Fraxinus spp.* (ash), can be useful for making the most of spring sunshine before there is need to shelter from high temperatures and bright light. Tree and shrub shelterbelts are discussed in chapter 5.

It is useful to have trees that provide a resource for different areas of the curriculum and ones that have different qualities to explore through the different senses. When deciding on new tree planting, or the management of existing trees, also consider their value in children's play. Trees that are distinctive because of unusual shape, colour or size can become 'characters' for children's play, creative writing or stories. Low branches make for easy climbing. Weeping trees can make good hideouts. To achieve these kinds of qualities it will be necessary to plant more natural forms of tree stock (rather than clean stemmed standard trees). There is a basic choice of planting young tree transplants or seedlings or older trees that

Oak leaves last well and are useful for teaching and play.

have not been shaped in the nursery (feathered or multi-stemmed trees). Wherever possible involve children in planning and implementing new tree planting. Using small transplants or seed will make it easier for them to be involved in the physical work.

There is enormous scope in school grounds for manipulating tree and shrub growth to create different effects. Cutting branches, and tying some together or to the ground can be a good way of making tunnels and dens and creating more interesting tree and shrub shapes and can be a fun way of involving the children. Willow sculpture is now a widespread activity and can be used to create shelters, 'houses', tunnels and other interesting shapes. Tree branches can be tied and trained to create overhead shelters. Leaving a central hole will create interesting patterns of light.

In most public situations tree leaves are considered a nuisance but in schools they can be real asset as a play material or a resource for sensory interest and teaching. Include some trees that have leaves that take a long time to decompose, such as *Fagus sylvatica* (beech), *Carpinus betulus* (hornbeam) and *Quercus spp.* (oak).

Trees, particularly mature ones, have a value for wildlife. Native trees tend to host the largest range of wildlife but exotic species can also provide useful food sources and/or nesting sites.

There are various safety issues to bear in mind. Some trees such as *Sorbus aucuparia* (mountain ash), *Populus spp.* (poplar) and *Tilia spp.* (lime) shed mucilaginous fruits or leaves and these should not be planted where they will overhang paths or hard surfaces. It is also advisable to avoid planting trees like *Taxus baccata* (yew) or *Laburnum spp.* that have toxic fruits or seeds in areas in easy access to children. Some trees have leaves which tend to cause skin rashes such as *Rhus typhina* (sumach) and these should also be avoided in frequently used areas.

Regular maintenance should include removal of branches that overhang paths at body height as these are

Even in winter, plants can give dramatic colour displays.

particularly hazardous for children with visual impairments (especially branches at head height). Branch removal and/or training may be needed for trees intended for climbing, perhaps removing mid range branches to limit the height to which children are able to climb or training lower branches to make them easier to reach. A deep bark mulch of approximately 100mm is perhaps the most natural looking safety surface to spread beneath climbing trees.

10.4 Plants for sensory interest

Designing for sensory interest is discussed in more detail in chapter 4d but it is useful here to explore some of the possibilities for selecting plants according to their different qualities. The following list is intended to offer ideas on the sorts of sensory experiences that can be provided and to give examples of plants. Plant selection will ultimately depend on site conditions and the size of plants wanted. Plant types are shown by different letters: **T** = tree, **s** = shrub, **G** = grass, **A** = annual, **H** = herbaceous perennial.

PLANTS FOR SOUND *Populus tremula* (aspen) **T**, *Eucalyptus spp.* (trunk) **T**, *Grasses* **H**, *Rhinanthus minor* (yellow rattle) **A**.

PLANTS FOR TEXTURE

    Feathery: *Robinia pseudoacacia* **T**, *Acer japonica* (Japanese maple) **T**, *Cotinus coggygria* **s**, *Sorbaria spp.***s**,

    Grasses: Ferns **H**.

    Spiky: *Yucca spp.***s**, *Phormium tenax* **s**, *Iris spp.***H**, *Crocosmia spp.***H**, *Grasses* **H**, Succulents **H**.

    Hairy: *Salix* buds (willow) **T**, *Alchemilla mollis* (lady's mantle) **H**, *Stachys lanata* (lamb's ears) **H**.

    Smooth: *Camellia japonica, Fatsia japonica, Sedum spectabile* (ice plant) **H**, *Bergenia cordifolia* (elephant's ears).

    Prickly: *Ilex aquifolium* (holly) **T**, *Olearia spp.* **s**, *Acanthus spinosus* **H**, *Dipsacus fullonum* (teasel) **H**

PLANTS FOR COLOUR

(Note that foliage provides colour all summer or all year, flowers provide only fleeting interest but can of course be valuable for seasonal effect).

    Red/purple foliage: *Fagus sylvatica purpurea* **T** (purple beech), *Cotinus coggygria* **s** , *Heuchera* 'Palace Purple' **H**.

    Yellow/gold foliage: *Robinia pseudoacacia* 'Frisia' **T** (false acacia), *Corylus avellana* 'Aurea' **s** (golden nut), *Philadelphus coronarius* 'Aureus' **s** (mock orange).

    White/gold variegated foliage *Acer negundo* **T** *Cornus alba* 'Elegantissima' **s**, *Eleagnus x ebbingei* 'Limelight' **s**, *Salvia officinalis* 'Variegata' **H**

    Silver/grey foliage: *Salix alba* **T** (white willow), *Sorbus aria* **T** (whitebeam), *Tilia tomentosa* **T** (silver lime), *Eleagnus angustifolia* **s**, *Buddleia spp.***s** *Artemesia spp.***H**

PLANTS FOR BARK INTEREST

    Coloured bark: *Salix alba* 'Chermesina' **T** (willow), *Betula spp.***T** (birch), *Cornus alba* **s** (dogwood), *Kerria japonica* **T**.

    Patterned bark: *Platanus x hispanica* **T** (plane), *Acer pennsylvanicum* **T** (snake bark maple).

    Textured bark: *Acer griseum* **T** (paperbark maple), *Prunus serrula* **T** (peeling bark).

    Plants with autumnm colour *Acer* **T** - many species (maple), *Prunus* **T** - some spp. (cherry), *Cotinus coggygria* **s** (smoke bush), *Sorbus aucuparia* **T** (mountain ash), *Cotoneaster spp.***s**.

CHARACTER PLANTS

    Unusual shapes: *Betula pendula* 'Youngii' **T** (weeping birch), *Tilia petiolaris* **T** (weeping lime), *Prunus amanogawa* **T** (lombardy cherry), *Salix matsudana* 'Tortuosa' **T** (contorted willow).

    Bold foliage: *Paulownia tomentosa* **T** (foxglove trees), *Fatsia japonica* **s** (Japanese aralia), *Vitis cognetiaec* (vine), *Ficus carica* **s** (fig), *Bergenia cordifolia* **H** (elephant's ears), *Gunnera manicata* **H**.

PLANTS FOR SCENT

Scented foliage:	*Eucalyptus spp.***T**, *Juglans spp.***T**, *Artemesia spp.***H**, *Geranium maccrorhizum* **H**, Herbs, Conifers.
Scented flowers:	*Malus hupehensis* **T**, *Fraxinus ornus* **T**, *Tilia spp.***T** (Lime), *Mahonia spp.***S**, *Viburnum* **S** - some species.
Scents associated with food:	*Cupressus macrocarpa* (Monterey cypress - pineapple), *Rosa rubiginosa* **S** (rose - apple), *Helichrysum serotinum* **H** (curry plant), *Mentha spicata* **H** (mint), *Cosmos sanguinea* **H** (chocolate plant).

PLANTS FOR FOOD *Juglans regia* **T** (walnut), *Malus sylvestris* **T** (apple), *Pyrus communis* **T** (pear), *Corylus avellana* **S** (hazel nut), *Fragaria vesca* **H** (alpine strawberry), Bush fruit.

PLANTS FOR WINTER INTEREST

Berries:	*Sorbus spp.***T**, *Rosa moyesii* **S**, *Cotoneaster spp.***S**, *Pyracantha spp.***S**, *Viburnum spp.***S**.
Catkins:	*Corylus avellana* **S** (hazel), *Salix spp.***TS** (willow), *Alnus spp* **T** (alder).

PLANTS THAT PRODUCE INTERESTING CONES, NUTS, SEEDS

*Pinus spp.***T** (pine), *Abies spp.***T** (fir), *Acer spp.***T** (maple), *Alnus spp.***T** (alder), *Castanea sativa* **T** (sweet chestnut), *Corylus avellana* **S** (hazel), *Dipsacus fullonum* **A** (teasel), *Scabiosa* **A** (paper moon), Sunflower **A**.

PLANTS FOR 'POPPING'   Balloon flower **A**, *Fuchsia spp.***S** Snapdragon **A**.

10.5 Hazardous plants

When selecting plants it is important to have a policy on plants that are poisonous, associated with allergies or asthma, thorny, produce unpleasant sap or that sting or scratch. The potential risk of including such plants in school grounds depends on the special needs of the children, the level of staff supervision and the location of the plants. Children who tend to put things into their mouths (and who can do this very quickly) are obviously most at risk from poisonous plants whilst children who have little perception of hazards and pain can be particularly vulnerable to thorny and stinging plants.

The issue of poisonous plants is not easy to resolve. Some plants have one or more parts that are highly toxic in small doses and there is little sense in including these. Especially hazardous are ones with attractive toxic parts, such as Laburnum. There are many more plants (including weeds that invade) with parts that are mildly poisonous and which either have to be eaten in large quantities for there to be an effect or which quickly induce vomiting. While it is sensible to restrict these to locations where they are out of reach of children if possible, it is often not realistic to try to completely eliminate them all from a site. For more information on poisonous plants refer to the references at the end of this chapter.

Plants can also be hazardous if they overhang access routes, especially for children who are unsteady on their feet or with visual impairments or if they obscure views of traffic (including bikes and cars). Careful plant selection is necessary to ensure that plants will not grow too tall or put out long extension growths over paths. Regular maintenance is also a key issue.

Plants that cause allergenic reactions are hard to sort out with great accuracy as there are some reactions which are individual and in some rare cases children can develop hyper-sensitivities to very low levels of contact. Plants with a reputation for causing reactions in many people should be avoided, for example Ruta graveolans and Rhus typhina. It will also be important to note any reactions to existing plants and remove as necessary, although identifying the cause can often be very difficult. There is also a danger of attracting wasps and bees in large numbers near the school building.

Asthma is increasingly common amongst children and the condition can be made worse by some plants. Again, reactions often vary from child to child but plants with high pollen release are best avoided, as indeed is work outside on days with a high pollen count. Strongly scented plants may cause problems with some children. Pollen from grasses is often highlighted as a problem and this may require keeping turf regularly mown (there are ways of having meadows by removing flowering grasses - see chapter 13). Information from children and their families is helpful in identifying potential problems.

10.6 Activities with plants

Plant recognition

These activities help children develop colour and shape perception and matching skills. Give children some different leaves and ask them to match them to trees or shrubs in the grounds. To make it more challenging use photocopied silhouettes of leaves. Use colour cards and ask children to find different flowers, leaves, berries etc that match different colours.

Seasonal recordings

To help children observe the changes in the landscape throughout the year, and to be more aware of the seasons, ask them to monitor plants that flower at different times and to make seasonal displays. These can include flowers, fruits, catkins and leaves.

Exploring textures

A wide range of textures can be explored using paper rubbings or plasticine which is pressed onto the surface. Consider bark, cones and leaves. Leaf textures can very from soft and furry to firm and smooth.

Leaf collecting

This is a good activity to do in autumn when tree leaves have fallen. Leaves can be used in art work, to make sculptures, graded into different sizes, shapes and colours or used as part of tree and shrub recognition.

Shaping plants

There are many options for sculpting plant material, for example shaping trees by tying and pruning branches, making tunnels and shapes out of willow by looping, tying and weaving branches. Cut material that is suitable for making large or small objects includes willow, dogwood, hazel, corn, bamboo and grasses.

Using plants to help develop numeracy skills

Plants provide endless possibilities for teaching numeracy skills from the basic level to highly complex tasks. The practical nature of the tasks can help reinforce the concepts taught in the classroom. A whole range of materials can be used, such as leaves, seeds, fruits, transplants, seedlings, crops and flowers. Activities include; arranging plant parts to illustrate different numbers, e.g. strawberries in ones, twos, threes; arranging six strawberries into the standard 3 x 2 arrangement and another six into a random pattern to show that both are the same number (helps relate number to spatial layout); collecting plant parts that resemble different numbers (a single tomato, a sycamore key with two seeds, a clover leaf with three parts etc; collecting leaves and grading them into different size groups (could also do for shape and colour); recording the number of objects in an area of the grounds (e.g. number of sunflowers, daffodil flowers, butterflies); showing the effects of addition and subtraction by having groups of apples and moving individual apples around; working out strategies for calculating the number of seeds in one sunflower head.

10.7   Sources of information

References

Food from your garden, 1977, Reader's Digest, London.

Plants for play, Robin Moore, 1993, MIG Communications, Berkeley, California.

Promoting nature in cities and towns. M. Emery. 1986. Croom Helm for Ecological Parks Trust (now Trust for Urban Ecology), London.

Danger in the garden, Val George, 1994, Growth Point, Horticultural Therapy, Somerset.

Poisonous plants in Britain and their effects on animals and man, Ministry of Agriculture, Fisheries and Food, HMSO, London.

The garden and the handicapped child, P. Elliott, Disabled Living Centre, London. (out of print)

There are many plant encyclopaedias that will give you information about the characteristics of different plants.

Organisations

Royal Horticultural Society, 80 Vincent Square, London, SW1P 2PE 0171 834 4333

National Asthma Campaign, Providence House, Providence Place, London N1 0NT. 0171 226 2260.

Royal Society for the Prevention of Accidents, Cannon House, The Priory, Queensway, Birmingham B4 6BS. 0121 200 2461.

HORTICULTURE

11

11.1 Introduction

There are many benefits that can come from involving children in growing and looking after plants. Children are encouraged to explore, touch and relate to living things and to use skills of decision making, problem solving and ingenuity. The wide range of plant types, activities and choice of indoor or outdoor working areas makes it valuable for the whole range of special needs and within all areas of the curriculum. Many schools find a real value in using horticulture for developing social and personal skills in children, for example for building self-esteem and confidence, increasing motivation and encouraging greater responsibility and independence. Garden areas can provide quiet and reassuring settings for counselling.

Many schools already involve children in growing and maintaining plants. Some have developed a child-scale school garden with a mix of cultivated land and containers, greenhouse and shed while others make use of existing beds within the school, containers or raised planters outside the classroom to carry out planting, pruning, weeding and watering. Some have taken advantage of large grounds to

The rewards of the harvest.

Children can develop socially, emotionally and intellectually through growing plants.

develop a horticulture project with polytunnel, greenhouse, potting shed, cultivated areas, fruit orchard, herb garden and raised planters.

Often the use of horticulture by people with special needs is termed 'horticultural therapy'. However, the term 'therapy' implies some form of rehabilitative effect and this is not necessarily appropriate here. Horticulture can be used to restore lost skills or to attain new ones or is widely used simply as a popular and motivating activity.

It is impossible in this publication to detail horticultural practice and reference should be made to the organisations and sources of information outlined at the end of this chapter. The following comments focus on the particular considerations that may be relevant in special schools.

11.2 Initial planning

The main challenge in planning a horticultural project is to achieve a balance between the educational aims, the horticultural practices required to achieve these aims and the abilities, needs and preferences of the children. It is important to have clear aims from the start and to make sure that these are realistic. In particular be clear about why you will be using horticulture and what you expect the main benefits to be. Be realistic and make sure that your plans are closely geared to the amount of time and range

Horticulture can provide an opportunity for a one-to-one session.

of tasks that staff and pupils will be able to manage. Also consider how the work will be covered during holidays.

In which areas of the curriculum will it be used and is there a commitment from the relevant members of staff to use the resources? Will the area also be used for recreational activities, as a setting for counselling or for training in work skills? You also need to decide when the resources are to be used. For example during the whole school year or fine weather only, how many hours each week and will this be a regular input? These will all have a bearing on the types of activity that will be appropriate.

What existing resources do you have already? For example do you have any funds for capital equipment, facilities such as outdoor buildings, materials and gardening or maintenance equipment. Consider the possibility of help from volunteers, parents and maintenance staff. What resources will you need immediately (for example, screening, shelter, shade, place to work during wet or cold weather, greenhouse, water, electricity or equipment)? How will running costs be met (for example from in-house funding, fund raising, donations or plant sales)?

11.3   Choosing a location

A major decision to make is where these horticultural activities are to be carried out. In some schools this depends largely on existing resources, such as beds and borders that can be planted and maintained and woodland that can be worked in. In other schools there may be scope for developing an area of the school grounds for a horticultural project. In either case, where resources are available, there is always the option of changing or ameliorating site conditions to make them more suitable. The following key issues and possible approaches should be considered.

A series of wooden framed boxes as an accessible cultivation system.

Access

*   Ensure there is good access within and around the site, from the school building and to toilets. Upgrade existing paths or build new ones, as required (see chapter 4).

*   Identify hazards to deal with immediately such as poisonous, prickly, stinging or allergenic plants, debris, glass, dangerous access and obstacles.

Climate

*   If the site is open to winds consider incorporating shelter belts, trellis, trees, walls and fences to create shelter and enclosure (see chapter 5).

*   If exposed to direct sunlight consider trees, pergolas and parasols to provide shade. There is also the option of working indoors or under cover.

Soil to cultivate

*   HEAVY CLAY SOILS: There are various options such as to avoid working when wet, add lots of bulky organic matter (e.g. spent mushroom compost or rotted manure), add lime or limit gardening activities to container growing.

The finished product.

*   STONY/GRAVELLY SOILS: Options are to stonepick, import soil, avoid growing root crops and/or choose plants that do not need extensive soil cultivation such as fruit trees and bushes.

- SANDY SOILS: Options are to add organic matter, use mulches, feed and irrigate often and/or choose plants that are tolerant of dry conditions.

- POORLY DRAINED OR WATERLOGGED SOILS: Options are to adjust topography or install drainage (try to determine if the barrier to drainage is on the soil surface or due to deeper layers as this will influence the form of drainage system required).

Soil pH can be measured using simple test kits from garden centres. Although these are often inaccurate they will give a rough indication. Most horticultural plants will perform adequately over a range of pH, from 5.5 - 7.5. Exceptions are the well known acid-loving species such as rhododendron and heather. Lowering the pH to suit these species is very difficult and they are best grown in separate containers. When conditions are too acid it is relatively easy to resolve by adding lime. Extremes of pH can lead to nutritional problems and these can sometimes be solved directly e.g. by applying sequestered iron fertiliser to alkaline soils.

Perennial weed infestation

It may be advisable to use herbicides to clean the site at the outset even if the long term aim is to avoid the use of chemicals. It is very difficult to control many perennial weeds, such as couch, by manual means especially where staff have other demands on their time.

Plastic sheet mulches may control some weeds but can only be used for some plants.

In woodland and natural areas it may be necessary to clear plants creating a hazard, such as brambles.

11.4 Planning activities

Planning activities is particularly important with horticulture as there is often a need to order materials or have plants ready for use. Some children will also benefit from being involved in planning, particularly autistic children who often depend on a sense of routine. The choice of activities will depend largely on the choice of plants to be grown but it is important to ensure that the tasks are appropriate for the children's abilities. Quite simply, if the activities are too difficult children will be unable to participate and if they are too easy children will quickly get bored. It is important to consider the following issues.

Task analysis

All horticultural operations can be broken down into series of component tasks, each requiring a different range of skills. For example, planting a tree may involve recognition and selection of appropriate tools, careful handling of transplant, digging hole to required depth, placing tree, filling hole and firming soil. This can be particularly useful for children who have problems with sequencing. However, it is important that a child is involved in the whole process even if s/he cannot actively participate in all the different stages. Otherwise there is a risk of individual tasks becoming unrelated to the ultimate goal.

Avoiding difficult tasks

When growing plants, try to avoid stages that are too difficult for children to be involved, unless staff and helpers are keen to spend evenings and weekends seed sowing or pricking out seedlings. There are often technical solutions. For example, seed sowing and pricking out require high levels of dexterity, hand to eye co-ordination and concentration and this often limits the number of children who can be involved. Ready-germinated seedlings are available in a range of sizes from most seed companies and it is also possible to buy individual small plants for potting on. This is also useful if there is no heated greenhouse space for early seed sowing or if there is limited growing space.

Activities like pricking out are good for developing dexterity and concentration.

Short-term projects

Try to include some activities that give quick results. These are useful for children with a short attention span or limited memory or to introduce horticulture as a new interest. Overactive children can also benefit from a series of short activities which change frequently, have clear targets which the children can achieve and be rewarded for. Examples include sprouting seeds such as cress and bean sprouts, planting up tubs and hanging baskets, pruning and shaping plants (pruning and coppicing can be useful ways of directing physical energy), using flowers and foliage in art work and planting trees and shrubs in the grounds.

Long-term projects

Medium or longer term projects are likely to form the bulk of the horticultural programme. These include a wide range of activities from field work through to class-room activities and many which involve a sequence of operations with an end re-sult. For example, from seed sowing to harvest or from designing landscape improvements through to their implementation. Children can be involved throughout

A fruit garden designed to be accessible to wheelchair users.

the whole sequence or at specific stages but it is important that they gain the final rewards of having helped produce something of quality.

Fitting in with the school year

It is important to select activities that can be achieved within the school year and for many schools this means avoiding plants that flower or produce their crop during the summer holiday when nobody is there to enjoy them.

Gourds grown on an overhead trellis are fun to look at and can be used later in the classroom,

Tough plants

Choose plants that are fairly robust and able to recover from damage or heavy pruning. Inexperience and poorly developed dexterity, co-ordination and balance are likely to result in rough handling and/or trampling of plants.

Multi-use plants

When selecting plants, consider a whole range of potential uses. For example, are there activities in art, design and technology or living skills that can use products such as dried flowers, herbs, willow canes, vegetables and fruits and fallen or coppiced wood? Plants with scent, textural and/or sound interest have an application in programmes aimed at developing sensory responses.

School grounds maintenance

Maintenance of the school grounds also provides a whole range of activities, such as grass cutting, pruning, weeding, woodland work, coppicing and tidying which might involve pupils. Some of this work involves the use of sharp tools and machinery and so is unlikely to be suitable for all pupils. Skills training and supervision will be especially important. It is also important to consider how these activities will fit in with existing maintenance arrangements; for example, will the maintenance work carried out by pupils be in addition to existing maintenance work (e.g. pruning and weeding) or will it replace some areas of existing work (e.g. grass cutting)? If the pupils are to be wholly responsible for some areas of grounds maintenance, what will happen during holiday periods?

Plants to avoid

Hazardous plants are discussed in 10.5. As a general principle it will be sensible to avoid poisonous plants, plants which thorns or spines or which produce irritant sap and plants that are commonly associated with allergies, skin rashes or asthma. Unless you can rely on additional help and expertise it will also be wise to avoid plants that are difficult or time consuming to grow.

11.5 Monitoring progress

It is a useful exercise to make a chart outlining a one year (or longer) programme. This should highlight the various operations to be carried out at different times of the year and will help identify potentially busy or quiet times.

It is a good idea to keep a record of activities in a diary or log book. Keeping a note of particular successes, or failures, will be a useful guide for the following year and will prevent repetition of mistakes. Add comments on how well the different activities met the needs of different children, how they could be modified next time, whether there were particular tasks that were a problem etc.

Children can use symbols, pictures and words to make a class or individual diary or work book. The types of plants, when they were sown/planted, weights/heights/sizes of harvested crops, methods used etc are all items that can be recorded and can form the basis of further class work in many different areas of the curriculum.

11.6 Equipment

There is an increasing range of proprietary equipment specially designed for disabled gardeners, particularly for those with physical disabilities or visual impairments. Items can be expensive, and not necessarily suitable for all children, but many are quite easy to make if you have access to a workshop and a skilled crafts person. Take care to ensure that DIY equipment is sufficiently robust and stable, without sharp corners or protrusions and gaps which can trap fingers, does not splinter and is suitable both for its horticultural role and the special needs of the children. Sources of advice and information on different types of equipment are given at the end of this chapter. The following list includes equipment which is commonly associated with horticultural projects in schools and outlines some key considerations.

Greenhouse

Choose one that will be large enough to accommodate a sufficient number of children. Consider access and select a model that has a wide door (or double doors) which is easy to open, has no trip rail at the entrance and has space inside for manoeuvring and working. Some models are designed to be wheelchair accessible (see chapter 7). If ordinary glass is likely to be a hazard, use safety glass or pvc.

Polytunnel

Select a robust, durable make and ensure that it is erected carefully and skilfully. Incorporate a hard path (sufficiently wide and level) to provide good access (internal

An accessible greenhouse: note the absence of threshold and the wide door.

soil paths tend to become uneven, slippery and boggy). When locating greenhouses or polytunnels, consider available light and risk of vandalism. If they are sufficiently large, chairs and tables can be included as a work area but bear in mind that there will be times when it is too hot, or too cold, for children to work there.

Tools

There is a wide range of adapted tools and equipment now available, including long handled and hand tools, equipment to assist with specific horticultural tasks (such as seed sowing), wheelbarrows and trolleys, watering equipment, etc. It is important to try a range of equipment to see which ones are useful for different children. Some modifications are easy DIY jobs, for example putting a length of tubular foam (sold as insulation for water pipes) over the handles of hand tools to make them easier for children with limited ability to grip and making rectangular wooden frames as planting guides for children with visual impairments. For further information see the references at the end of the chapter.

There is an enormous range of special equipment now available.

Storage

It is important to have somewhere to store tools, equipment, work clothes and materials, preferably a shed which is specifically for this purpose. This can be organised as an additional educational resource, for example by having specific places for different tools marked by a painted outline of their shape or by a symbol and/or name.

Raised planters and containers

These are often used to bring plants up to a height where they can be reached by wheelchairs or children who find it

difficult to work at ground level. They are also a useful addition or alternative to

Picture labels help children identify different seed containers.

growing plants in the open ground. They have the advantage that they can be located close to the building, which makes access easier and makes it possible for different classes to have their own planters. Regular watering and feeding will be necessary. Additional features can be added, such as trellis for climbing plants, tool holders, hand rails and grips for support. It is also useful to build in, or have alongside the planter, shelves and tables to provide a working area and somewhere to put tools, materials, drinks etc.

Raised planter with space for wheeelchairs to work face on.

Dimensions and details of planters are critical to ensure that they are comfortable to work at and do not encourage bad posture. Dimensions will need to relate to the heights and working positions of the children who are to use them and an ideal approach is to measure children to work out an appropriate range of planter sizes (this may be a good class exercise). Planters to be used from a standing position must have toe holes. Children in wheelchairs will garden from a sideways position and will not be able to reach far across the soil surface so a narrow planter, or one that can be accessed from both sides, will be required.

Staging enables easy access to plants and is easy to build.

Some planters have a shallow lip which enables a wheelchair user to work face on with the bulk of the chair under the lip. The disadvantage is that the shallow soil layer is prone to drying out fast and the limited root space reduces the range of plants which can be grown.

Watering equipment

Watering is one of the most complex of all horticultural tasks as it requires an enormous range of skills in order to do the job properly. Hence the numbers of people who lose plants through under- or over-watering. It is a job that will require supervision but there is also some equipment which can make the task easier and reduce the risks of losing plants. Capillary matting, seep hoses and sprinklers offer alternatives or, more likely, back ups to hand watering. Using a hose with a fine spray nozzle will reduce the risk of plants being washed out of pots and makes the job possible for children who are not strong enough to carry watering cans. Try not to remove completely the opportunity for children to do some watering - it is an fundamental part of nurturing plants and is a task from which many children get a lot of pleasure.

Large tractor tyres - low cost containers.

Watering is made easier by fixing a hose reel to a wall.

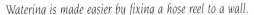

11.7 Indoor horticultural activities

Potting bulbs

This is a useful activity for autumn when outdoor activity is often restricted by the weather. The activity is suitable for a wide range of abilities. Reliable types include Daffodils (particularly some of the miniature ones such as Tete a Tete, Pipit, Minnow), Hyacinth, Paperwhite Narcissus, Dwarf tulips e.g. *T. greigii & T. batalinii*, *Iris reticulata* and *Amaryllis*.

Re-potting plants

Many plants can now be bought very small (in 9cm pots) and these provide ideal material for potting on. The plants are large enough to tolerate a certain amount of rough handling but small enough for children to still feel that they are 'growing the plant'. For example, houseplants in 9cm pots, cost approx. 90p each. Select fast growing, reliable species such as *Philodendron*, *Ficus*, *Ivy*, *Tradescantia*, *Schefflera* and transplant them into 1 litre pots. Young shrubs and herbaceous perennials can be bought as '"liners" for about 40p each and transplanted into 1 litre pots. These can be either grown outside or in a polytunnel.

Pressing flowers

A wide range of flowers can be pressed and later used in craft activities such as making greetings cards, gift tags and bookmarks. A good continuity theme can be developed if the flowers are grown outside, collected and pressed and then used to create an attractive final product.

Drying flowers and herbs

There are other activities which link with outdoor horticultural work. Dried flowers can be used to sell in bunches, to make arrangements, or for making potpourri. Flowers and foliage can also be preserved using glycerine. Dried herbs can be packaged and sold, given as presents or used for cooking. Some can be used as part of other craft activities such as making lavender bags.

Making plant labels

This can be incorporated into garden planning sessions or as an activity in itself. With children who cannot write, pictures of plants can be used instead although they will need waterproofing by covering with plastic.

Fresh flower arranging

This can involve simply putting cut flowers and foliage into a vase through to using Oasis and maybe even Ikebana. Again this can link with the outdoor activities of growing the flowers and harvesting.

Festive decorations

A whole host of possibilities with plant material present themselves in association with festivals. Children can plan celebrations which may involve collecting plant material such as flowers, berries, leaves, cones, twigs, and berries to make decorations (both outdoor and indoor). Possibilities include harvest festival and religious festivals and new year celebrations of different countries.

Growing indoor plants

Indoor plants (if healthy) help to create a more attractive environment for children and staff. Many children also enjoy the chance to grow houseplants. Plants should be carefully selected to suit the situation, in particular the amount of light and risk of frost damage. In most interiors, away from windows, there is insufficient light to grow well a very wide range of plants and if a more exciting range is desired supplementary lighting must be provided (there is a wide range of lights now available for indoor horticulture).

Using plants as dyes

This usually causes a great deal of interest. It can be done on plain pieces of un-treated cotton or silk cloth and even more exciting results can be achieved from tie-dyeing or batik. Plant dyeing can also linked with other crafts such as the spinning and weaving of wool.

Planning gardening activities through the year

One of the educational benefits of gardening is the need to plan ahead. The planning process can give children a sense of purpose, a greater feeling of responsibility and control and something to look forward to. This is a useful winter activity although can be done at any time of year. Garden books and/or plant catalogues and old calendars with pictures of plants can be used to identify plants within a particular theme (e.g. for a wildlife area, herb garden, or seasonal display). Children can select plants, cut out or draw pictures, make labels and prepare a plant list with prices and firms where they can be purchased (depending on appropriate skill level). Further options include selecting plants with scent, berry, leaf colour for different times of the year, dividing the year into seasons or months to introduce the challenge of a time-scale and identifying crops which can be grown or harvested at different times (remember to avoid school holidays).

11.8 Outdoor horticultural activities

Plant sales

Plant sales can help to encourage local people, families and friends to come into the school and promote a positive image. Children see that what they have grown is valued by other people and have the opportunity to practice social skills as well as numeracy skills associated with handling money and quantities of produce.

Planting a raised planter or large container

If well designed, raised planters provide easy access to plants and can also allow individual children or groups to have their own small, defined area to garden. Initial planning sessions help involve children in the whole process and might involve deciding what plants to include and working out dimensions for the planters (children can measure each other, draw plans, calculate soil volumes).

A vegetable garden using mini-veg varieties

Mini-veg varieties are useful because they have a shorter growing season and so can be fitted in to the school term more easily (rather than maturing during the summer holiday). They can also be sown at closer spacings which makes them good for small spaces and raised planters. With careful planning you can have activities year round (outside mid winter). The activity can include initial planning with the children, sowing seeds into modular trays (using large seeded or pelleted seed for children with limited grip or dexterity), labelling trays, raising seedlings in a greenhouse or on a window sill, watering, transplanting to planting site, harvesting and recording weights and lengths of produce, calculating totals and averages.

Growing 'themes'

Some schools have found that introducing extra challenges or themes can help stimulate and sustain children's interest in growing plants. For example, hold a competition (between individuals or classes) to grow the tallest sunflower, the longest runner bean, the heaviest pumpkin, the biggest marrow, the greatest number of potatoes in a container or number of tomatoes from one plant. Such activities can involve a multitude of skills in planning, maintenance and harvest.

Activities to develop language skills

Horticulture can provide a relaxed setting for conversation and discussion with the advantage that some children communicate more freely than they would in a more formal classroom setting. Activities and settings can also be stimuli for creative writing and can help children develop an understanding of instructions. Learning language can be more effective as children learn through a combination of senses and practical activities allow children to hear a word, see and use the object and to see the word written (as text or Makaton or Rebus symbols). Labels alongside tools in a storage shed or on seed containers can help reinforce such learning.

11.9 Sources of information

References

Able to Garden, Peter Please, 1990, Horticultural Therapy, Somerset

Children's gardening, Peter Please, 1991, Horticultural Therapy, Somerset.

Gardening and the handicapped child, Pat Elliot, 1978, Disabled Living Foundation.

Gardening is for everyone, A. Cloet & C. Underhill, 1990, Human Horizon Series, Souvenir Press.

Gardening without sight, Kathleen Fleet, 1989, RNIB, London.

Growing with gardening - a 12 month guide for therapy, recreation and education, B. Moore, 1989, University of North Carolina Press, Chapel Hill & London.

Intensive vegetable production for mentally handicapped people, Peter Thoday & Rosemary Dodd, 1988, Federation to Promote Horticulture for Disabled People, Dorset.

Raised planters, Nick Rowson and Peter Thoday, 1980, University of Bath.

Sharing nature with children, Joseph Cornell, 1978, Exley Publications.

The garden and the handicapped child, P. Elliott, 1978, Disabled Living Foundation, London. (Out of print but can be obtained through libraries).

Therapeutic horticulture, Rosemary Hagedorn, 1987, Winslow Press.

Organisations

American Horticultural Therapy Association, 362A Christopher Avenue, Gaithersburg, Maryland, 20879, USA. (USA) 301 948 3010

Community Gardening Projects Scotland, 4 Drum Street., Edinburgh EH17 8QG. 0131 664 2335

The Horticulture for All Thorngrove Centre, Common Mead Lane, Gillingham, Dorset SP8 4RE. 01747 822242

Gardening for Disabled Trust, The Secretary, Hayes Farmhouse, Hayes Lane, Peasmarsh, Rye, East Sussex TN31 6XR. 01424 882345

Mary Marlborough Centre, Nuffield Orthopaedic NHS Trust, Windmill Road, Headington, Oxford OX3 7LD. 01865 227600

Horticultural Therapy, Goulds Ground, Vallis Way, Frome, Somerset BA11 3DW. 01373 464782

People-Plant Council, Virginia Polytechnic Institute & State University, Department of Horticulture, Blacksburg, Virginia 24061-0327, USA. 001 703 231 6254

A sensory garden incorporating seating.

DESIGNING FOR ANIMALS

12

12.1 Introduction

The city farm movement has demonstrated the huge benefits that children can gain from contact with animals. Benefits that are often highlighted centre on the response of children to animals and how this can help to teach issues such as care, responsibility and an awareness of the different stages of life, and issues such as sex, illness and death. Many children with illness or disability have spent their lives being looked after, and having decisions made for them, by other people. Looking after an animal can help a child understand the importance of commitment and responsibility for another life. Some children who have suffered abuse find it hard to trust people or to form relationships. Many such children find animals a non-threatening and rewarding focus of attention.

Keeping animals in schools is a commitment that shouldn't be taken lightly. They require regular feeding and cleaning out and there are costs involved in constructing housing, buying food and covering vet's bills. Weekends and holidays can be a problem, particularly for non-residential schools. Some schools manage by having a rota which includes pupils but some find that wide catchment areas and the fact that their pupils have limited mobility make this difficult.

12.2 Opportunities for contact with animals

Large animals, such as sheep, donkeys and goats, are only options for schools with extensive grounds, access to sufficient husbandry knowledge and adequate maintenance commitment. It is often necessary to select animals which have a good temperament and can tolerate some clumsy handling. City farms will be a good point of contact for sourcing animals. Some schools have farm units which involve children in a wide range of husbandry operations, such as feeding, cleaning out, grooming, sheep shearing and collecting eggs. Outdoor buildings and facilities can be designed to be accessible for children with physical disabilities, for example nesting boxes at a height where children using wheelchairs can collect the eggs. Interpretative materials can use written information, pictures, tactile information, Braille, Makaton or Rebus symbols or audio aids, as appropriate.

Animals are a popular feature in this residential school.

Small animals, such as rabbits and guinea pigs, require less space and are small enough for a child's lap. Cages can be brought indoors and can be set at waist height so that children using wheelchairs can see the animals. Fish in tanks and birds in aviaries can be interesting to watch but obviously do not offer the same level of response. Dogs and cats are popular with children and can offer a real sense of companionship.

> "Contact with animals is highly therapeutic for many children with emotional and behavioural difficulties. However, their uncontrolled behaviour means that it is not safe to have animals permanently on site. Staff bring their dogs in often, and the children become familiar with them without the possibility of injury to the animal."

Often these belong to staff, in which case holidays and weekends are not a problem. Small caged animals can also be taken home to cover such periods. There is a note of caution with small animals; they are more vulnerable to harm so consider carefully whether any children are likely to mistreat them or handle them too roughly. Some schools have avoided small caged animals, limiting choice to pets such as dogs that remain with the staff or animals that are able to "escape" to a safe refuge.

Visits to nearby city farms or commercial farms gives children the chance to see a wider range of animals and to learn about their upkeep. Most sites encourage children to touch animals and some offer horse riding, tractor rides and the option of helping with farm jobs.

Horse riding is enjoyed by many children and can help develop skills of independence, co-ordination, balance and posture. For children who find mobility a constant struggle, horse riding can offer an enormous sense of freedom. It is unlikely that many schools will have sufficient space, and particularly sufficient finance, to have their own horses but there are many 'Riding for the Disabled' centres across the country. In Hampshire there is a scheme that focuses on the needs of children with diabetes and has a strong therapeutic aspect to its work. For schools with large grounds, it is sometimes possible to arrange for horses to be brought to the school site.

12.3   Sources of information

Organisations

Riding for the Disabled Association, Avenue 'R', National Agricultural Centre, Stoneleigh, Kenilworth, Warwickshire CV8 2LR. 01203 696510

National Federation of City Farms, 93 Whitby Road, Brislington, Bristol BS4 3QF. 0117 9719109

Farming & Wildlife Advisory Group, National Agricultural Centre, Stoneleigh, Kenilworth, Warwickshire, CV8 2RX. 01203 696699.

DESIGNING FOR NATURE

13

13.1 Introduction

Many children respond positively to wildlife, finding it a constant source of fascination. Wildlife can be an excellent motivator and it is often possible to achieve responses from children more effectively than from more formal strategies. There are many reports, particularly from the USA, that show how the behaviour and attitudes of 'disruptive' children have been transformed by nature programmes.

An aspect that is often highlighted in environmental education is that natural areas are visually complex and may stimulate mental skills in deciphering and discriminating. The understanding that the natural world is not controlled can also provide a heightened sense of mental freedom for some children. The element of surprise and thrill can evoke spontaneous and increased responses.

As with everything, problems can occur. For children who are easily overwhelmed, or who have had little experience of the natural world, wildlife areas may be a source of anxiety or disinterest. For some children this may require a more gradual introduction to the subject but for others the topic will simply not be effective. Staff can also have reservations about using wildlife areas for teaching, often based on fears over safety. A clear school policy on health and safety and supervision, good design and regular maintenance are important to allay such worries.

Nature is a constant source of fascination for many children.

Children learning to cooperate through a wildlife project.

Woodland sign giving clear, pictorial information.

There is an enormous range of activities that can be developed under the theme of nature and there are many texts that outline ideas. These books are not generally aimed at children with special needs but the practical and multi-sensory content of many of the activities makes them easily adaptable for a wide range of children. There will obviously need to be application of these different activities within the appropriate areas of the curriculum.

13.2 Design requirements

Children with special needs generally have few opportunities for more than cursory contact with nature. Access is a key issue and the main challenge is to create good access without destroying the character of the natural area. The materials used for paths and hard areas should be in keeping with the surrounding areas and there is particular value in using them in an imaginative way. Options are discussed in more detail in chapter 4.

If the grounds are large enough it is a good policy to include wildlife areas for children to go into as well as areas which remain undisturbed. Some wildlife species can become very tolerant of disturbance and noise if this is regular and if they come to recognise that it is not threatening. This applies to many different birds and to squirrels. It is therefore a good idea to make sure that regular activities are scheduled so that the animals will get used to them. However, there will also be a group of species that remain shy of people and these will benefit from relatively undisturbed areas. It is worth noting that there is a real value from not being able to see some species very often - both children and staff can get a tremendous thrill from seeing the occasional fox, badger or deer for example.

There is a common misapprehension in schools that wildlife gardens and nature areas are providing wildlife habitats. In reality there are relatively few species that are able to survive within the confines of school sites; most of

Boardwalk paths giving good access and harmonising with natural settings.

the large animals will need wider territories than any one site alone can provide. Wildlife gardens often really function as 'feeding stations'. This is an excellent strategy, particularly for children with limited mobility, as it means that wildlife activity can be 'brought to the children'. Again, there are strategies appropriate to different species. Some wildlife, including many birds, will become tolerant of people and will come for food even if children are nearby and it may be possible to encourage hand feeding. Other species will not get used to people and it will be necessary to view them from indoors or from a hide.

The usual aim of wildlife projects is to encourage as wide a range of animals as possible. To achieve this requires a lot of structural complexity (shrub masses, open areas, wooded areas etc), an overall mosaic of habitats (grasslands, ponds, woodland, hedges etc) and as many different plants as possible. It is sensible to focus primarily on native species but include some exotics to provide extra resources. The most valuable are those that produce lots of flowers with nectar, lots of berries, and those that give evergreen shelter. Shelter is also important for insects as there are many that will be deterred by a windy site. Also avoid making a site too tidy -

A nature strip outside the classroom provide resources within easy reach.

dead wood, tree stumps and old trees etc. provide valuable habitats. It is a good idea to keep some grass long through the winter rather than cutting it all in late summer. Insects can be encouraged by relatively simple means. These 'mini-beast' habitats are familiar to most schools and include rock and wood piles and pieces of old carpet or wood which can be lifted every so often to look for mini-beasts.

An easy-to-make classroom bird hide.

13.3 Features

Hides

Hides can be an excellent way of giving children the chance to secretly view and listen to the natural world.

Bird hides (wheelchair accessible) give children the chance to spy on nature.

They are also a good way of focusing children's attention and encouraging them to look and discover for themselves. Hides can easily be designed to accommodate wheelchairs where the key issues are ensuring level access into the hide through a sufficiently wide door, manoeuvring space inside and windows at an appropriate height. Ideally, a series of hides will be provided in different settings so that the sounds and views from each will be different. Binoculars can be mounted on supports to help children with limited arm movement, limited strength or poor motor control.

Tree platforms

Platforms built into a mature tree canopy offer a captivating experience to any child, but particularly to a child who has never been able to climb a tree. Access to the platform is normally by ladder but to make the experience available to all children a hoist could be fitted. Low level platforms are useful for children (and staff!) who would rather not venture to the top. Safety is a key issue and particular attention should be paid to the safety and life expectancy of the tree, the appropriateness of the design and the quality and durability of the construction and materials. Where there are slopes schools may be lucky enough to have an option where level access can be provided directly into the tree canopy. Another approach is to build a raised platform at a height that takes it alongside the canopies of small or medium trees, as seen at Mcldreth Manor School (see 14.4).

Seating and picnic tables

The freedom of children to use wildlife areas for recreation during break times will largely depend on the ease of supervision but ideally there will be some spaces where this is possible. Where possible provide seats in as many different settings as possible. In woodlands, fallen tree trunks and cut logs will provide seats for some children. Provide some clear spaces where wheelchairs can park alongside seats.

Bird/bat boxes

These have the obvious value of providing nesting sites for wildlife but they also have a real value in making it possible to know where birds and bats are nesting so that children can

Platform built around a mature tree.

watch them. Where appropriate, locate some boxes within view of classroom windows.

Ponds

Ponds are a great attraction to most children. If well designed, they can provide a wealth of educational material. The most common mistake with pond construction is to make them too small with the result that they support minimal wildlife and are particularly vulnerable to over-heating and drying out. Larger ponds are more successful in both wildlife and visual terms. Safe access to pond water is a prime issue and the best solution is to provide a hard edge on at least one side. If the pond is sufficiently large, a boardwalk over the water will allow access to deeper areas of the

Ponds are a rich teaching resource.

A *dipping platform for wheelchair users.*

pond. Providing a hard surface ramp that runs into the water may allow children who use wheelchairs to experience wet feet. The value of a pond for wildlife is very dependent on the design and management of the edges. Options for providing good access should therefore be balanced with the need to keep some parts of the pond perimeter more natural and out-of-bounds. Remember also that amphibians and many birds rely on the right type of habitat around a pond; there may be a value in providing rock piles for newts for example. An isolated pond surrounded by mown grass is a wasted opportunity. As a safety precaution, ponds are usually fenced to control access to the water but there is no need for this to diminish the visual qualities of the pond. A square fence in short grass will look more like a compound than part of an attractive landscape feature. Shrub plantings and earth moulding can help to reduce the impact of fencing, especially if these are continued outside the fence so as to avoid a sharp boundary between the 'pond zone' and the rest of the landscape.

Grassland

Many schools have meadow areas in their school grounds. These provide useful educational material but can also provide different play and sensory experiences. Grass mazes can be created very simply by a lawn mower (if the grass is not very long) or by a strimmer and can be an effective way of combining play and orientation skills.

If pollen is likely to be a problem (for children with asthma) it is still possible to have a meadow by cutting the sward when the grasses are flowering and putting a focus on early summer flowers, such as bulbs, primroses, cowslips. It may also be possible to add some autumn interest although the

The mower can be used to create temporary patterns in grass.

options are more limited, e.g. colchicum, some crocus and cyclamen under trees. Accessibility on grass can be a problem for wheelchairs but there are proprietary systems available for reinforcing turf to make it more suitable, for example by sowing the grass on a substrate containing a high proportion of sand or gravel or a mixture of soil and shredded rubber.

13.4 Maintenance

The management of nature areas will have a direct influence on the range of plant and animal species. For example, a grass meadow which is cut in May will have a different composition of plant species to one which is cut in late summer and this in turn will determine the range of insects which can feed on it. Decisions concerning maintenance will also be influenced by the abilities of the children and the particular aims of the programme. For example, woodland work may be seen as an excellent means of developing skills in team work, communication and physical development and there may be a deliberate policy of introducing a labour intensive form of maintenance, such as coppicing, thinning, planting and monitoring. The main aim is to maximise opportunities for appropriate maintenance tasks but to limit work that is too difficult for children to do.

13.5 Activities with nature

Bird watching

Watch from a hide in the grounds or a classroom hide. Give bird lists (names, symbols or pictures) to children so that they can tick different birds as they see them. This can link with classroom activities such as preparing graphs, reports, drawing pictures, looking up information from books or on the computer.

Exploring the world of mosses and lichens

These plants tend to go relatively unnoticed in the landscape but they offer a range of colour and texture that is hard to equal in other plant groups. They reflect subtle variations in soil type, moisture levels and shade and many types can be found growing in specific places. Children can learn how lichens have been traditionally used as dye materials and can use magnifying glasses and microscopes to see just how complex and fascinating these plant structures are. Be careful not to be too destructive with these activities - it can take a long time for lichens to grow. Mosses can survive under very dry conditions and often show an amazing ability to rapidly expand and change colour when water is applied.

Making wildlife boxes and hides is an easy and absorbing activity.

Animal tracks

This is a very easy yet exciting activity. Tracks are easiest to find in soft soil or in snow but you may be able to set up a surface specially to show where animals have walked. You need to anticipate where there are likely to be animals (such as field mice, voles, rabbits, hedgehogs, badgers, foxes, deer) and put down a layer of wet sand for larger, heavier animals or dry dust for smaller creatures. Leave it overnight and go back in the morning to see what tracks have been left. You might run a competition where children guess what the animals are going to be. You will need a book which tells you how to identify different tracks, unless you are already skilled in this. This can link with other activities, such as studying the life histories of animals, drawing and painting, craft work, visits to wildlife centres etc.

A nature mobile

Children can collect up to eight objects which they take back to the classroom and make a mobile from them. This can help children remember a particular trip and encourages them to focus more on small details.

Looking at detail

Give children a small quadrate (e.g. 500mm x 500mm) or hoop and ask them to place it on an area or object (e.g. tree bark, woodland floor, grass). Ask them to focus on that small space, to observe the detail and to draw and describe the different things they see.

Night time

Studying wildlife during the night is likely to be more of an option for a residential school or as part of a study trip or when camping. There are many options such as exploring night sounds (using tape recorders), looking at the stars and collecting insects. Many of the larger wild animals feed at night and might be encouraged to come near a hide or window.

Designing and making bird feeders

Many children find wildlife fascinating so this activity can help stimulate their interest, while encouraging them to plan and be creative and to develop physical skills. This is a useful winter activity although it can be done at any time of year. Some schools have found it very successful with children with emotional and behavioural difficulties. Try to include a wide range of feeders to attract different birds. Position feeders where they can be seen from a bird hide or classroom hide so that they can be monitored by the children to record the number and types of bird that visit them. They can compare the success of different feeders, positions and foods. Possible types include wooden bird tables, coconut half, trays placed on the ground, mesh feeders from vegetable or nut bags. For children with limited dexterity, the activity can be limited to a simple feeder (e.g. mesh or coconut half) and materials prepared so that they can do the remaining task - e.g. filling the mesh with peanuts or looping string through the coconut half.

Outwitting the squirrels

If you have squirrels in the grounds they are likely to be attracted by bird feeders. Children can be given the challenge of designing feeders that cannot be used by squirrels. This can be run as a competition or as a group activity.

13.6   Sources of information

References

A *guide to habitat creation*. C. Baines & J. Smart. 1991. London Ecology Unit, London.

How to make a wildlife garden. C. Baines. 1984. Elm Tree Books, London.

Promoting nature in cities and towns. M. Emery. 1986. Croom Helm for Ecological Parks Trust (now Trust for Urban Ecology), London.

Informal countryside recreation for disabled people. Countryside Commission, 1994. CC, Cheltenham.

Flora for fauna. J. Hamilton & P. Hart (eds). 1995. The Linnean Society, London.

Discovering wildlife. A directory of wildlife sites suitable for people with a disability. The Sensory Trust. 1996. The Sensory Trust, Swindon.

The series of practical publications by British Trust for Conservation Volunteers, Oxon.

These include:

Drystone Walling; *Footpaths*; *Grasslands*; *Hedging*; *Sand dunes*; *Wetlands*; *Woodlands*.

Organisations

The British Butterfly Conservation Society, P.O. Box 222, Dedham, Colchester, Essex CO7 6EY. 1206 322342

British Trust for Conservation Volunteers, 36 St. Mary's Street, Wallingford, Oxon OX10 0EU. 01491 39766.

Centre for Environmental Interpretation, Metropolitan University of Manchester, Lower Chatham Street, Manchester, M15 6BY. 0161 247 1067

Countryside Commission, John Dower House, Crescent Place, Cheltenham, Glos GL50 3RA. 01242 521381.

Farming and Wildlife Advisory Group, National Agricultural Centre, Stoneleigh, Kenilworth, Warwickshire CV8 2RX 01203 696699

The Fieldfare Trust, 67a The Wicker, Sheffield S3 8HT. 01742 701668.

Forestry Commission, 231 Corstorphine Road, Edinburgh EH12 7AT. 0131 334 0303.

Royal Society for the Protection of Birds, The Lodge, Sandy, Bedfordshire SG19 2DL. 01767 80551.

The Sensory Trust, Swindon Environment Centre, 47b Fleet Street, Swindon, SN1 4RE 01793 526244

WATCH, The Green, Witham Park, Waterside South, Lincoln LN5 7JR. 01522 544400

CASE STUDIES

14

The following case studies have been chosen from the many schools visited to give inspirational examples of school grounds projects. Above all they are living testaments to the fact that what is written in this book can be achieved.

14.1 Kelvin School, Glasgow

Kelvin School is located in the centre of Glasgow and, as in most special schools, the children come from a wide catchment area. An innovative series of school grounds developments was initiated to improve the appearance of the school and to provide interest and educational opportunities for children with visual impairments. Initial planning identified three phases; a garden area, a maze and a shelter. Funding was received from Esso when the school was 'adopted' by an Esso oil tanker and a brick 'tanker' was built in the garden to celebrate; it is named after the sponsoring tanker. Help with construction and materials came from Anniesland College, the rangers at Mugdock Country Park and the gardener at St Andrew's College.

> Special school catering for approximately 40 children. All children have visual impairments and many also have learning difficulties and other disabilities.

The children were involved at all stages of the projects. They designed the garden, with teachers helping to decide what was practical and feasible, and the maze was a joint effort between the pupils and Anniesland College. There was a great value for all in the planning and design stages and the results are aesthetically pleasing.

The projects include features for tactile and scent interest and include Braille labels.

> "The children love it and have developed a real interest in the environment. They are proud of their school and have a real sense of ownership".

All areas are wheelchair accessible. The developments were built to last. The garden is used in all areas of the curriculum. Food crops, herbs and flowers are grown and a variety in plant material, hard detailing and sculpture provide a basis for creative writing and poetry, art and design. In the early stages designs and plans were prepared and invitations to the garden opening were done on computer. Plays have been staged outside with environmental themes, festivals and topics have been studied and there have been numerous activities involving numeracy, communication and perception skills. The grounds are also widely used for the informal curriculum through play, exploration and the imaginative use of features, for example the play 'tanker' is always surrounded by sharks.

Maintenance of the project areas is carried out by school staff and pupils. Each class has responsibility for one particular area of the grounds. Holidays are difficult but the janitor covers essential work (mainly watering) and there is a blitz of activity at the beginning of the autumn term. Although the project is largely due to the enthusiasm and commitment of one teacher, all staff are now involved and this is important to ensure longterm success.

> "The school itself will probably fall down before the garden and maze".

14.2 Loddon School, Hampshire

In common with many special schools, Loddon is not a purpose-built site but an adaptation of a former residential property. The school therefore inherited a 'domestic style' landscape which provided few opportunities for the children. The basic structure and style of the extensive grounds have been retained but the school has implemented a series of imaginative changes to provide a range of opportunities to meet the various needs of the children. Development has been planned as a 'circular' series of areas and features and has made good use of existing resources. Projects include a music garden (the result of a student project by a music therapist), fitness trail (built along the course of an existing water feature), adventure play areas, animal paddocks, small gardens, tree planting and barbecue.

Residential School for 22 children, aged between 8-19, with emotional and behavioural difficulties and severe and profound learning difficulties, visual impairments, autism and language disabilities. In particular, many of the children exhibit severely challenging behaviour and many

"It gives our children a sense of freedom that they don't normally enjoy. Although they are not physically disabled they are very handicapped by their lack of social behaviour skills. Because of the nature of their disability parents generally need to restrict opportunities for these children. So we see huge changes in children when they come here and can explore open spaces."

The school is committed to using and developing the grounds and recognises enormous benefits to the education and quality of life of the children. The grounds are regularly used for walking, play, picnics, sport, bikes, exercise, sitting, music, storytelling and social events. The children are physically very active so opportunities for exercise are important. The extensive grounds were felt to be essential for a residential school with this type of client group. Social events include family days, May Day processions, bonfire processions, multicultural days and theatre events.

All staff and children have gardening timetabled into their weekly programmes and there are plans to develop horticulture. There is occasional involvement of people from the local community, particularly with project development.

The grounds are maintained by two full time maintenance staff. There are also maintenance sheets on which staff note any problems which require attention. These are sent to the estates manager each day and it is his responsibility to implement remedial action. This is an excellent way of sharing responsibility for identifying and dealing with maintenance problems as they arise.

14.3 The Royal School for the Deaf, Manchester

Four years ago the extensive school grounds offered few opportunities for the students. School grounds improvements were initiated to change this and to open up possibilities for using the grounds as part of the school's curricula. The result has been an inspirational series of developments creating a richly stimulating environment accessible to all.

Initially a feasibility study was commissioned to identify options and to safeguard against expensive mistakes. A plan was subsequently prepared. Help with funding and development came from various sources, in particular the Willow Trust, British Aerospace, the Business Enterprise Scheme, the Cheshire Landscape Trust and Manchester Metropolitan University. A particular emphasis was placed on sensory experiences and the development of practical and self help skills.

The projects have included tree and shrub planting to provide shelter around the perimeter and to divide large expanses into a series of smaller spaces and different habitats. Age-related play opportunities include an infant and junior play space, adventure play areas and an assault course. A sensory path incorporates different hard surfaces to indicate particular adjacent areas. A sensory garden has raised beds, different sorts of paving, a seasons garden, water feature, trellis for hanging things (musical instruments, clay tiles, decorations etc) and removable trellis panels. A horticultural project includes a polytunnel, greenhouse and vegetable garden. Willow domes, created by the Willow Trust, are outdoor classrooms and recreation spaces. Other features include mounds for rolling down, dens, meeting places and seats.

The Royal School for the Deaf has approximately 120 pupils between the ages of 5 to 26. All students have hearing impairments and most have multiple disabilities, particularly physical disabilities, profound learning difficulties, visual impairments and emotional and behavioural difficulties. Students come from all over the UK and many are residential.

"The pupils are most likely to succeed when they are involved in 'doing' activities rather than academic learning. Environmental education is an ideal activity learning medium".

Children have been involved in as many stages as possible. The developments are ongoing and a masterplan identifies ideas and aims for the future. These include further planting, more habitats, a sunburst maze, a track on the perimeter, some mounds and more paths to access the different areas.

Projects have been carefully planned and there has been an emphasis on good robust construction to ensure that facilities are durable and safe. Grounds maintenance is carried out by the existing grounds staff and care was taken during the planning stage to identify the maintenance requirement associated with any new features. The sensory garden and raised beds in the infant and junior playground are to be maintained by the children to help them develop motor skills. The organisation and supervision of these activities is the responsibility of the teachers and special support assistants.

14.4 Meldreth Manor School, Hertfordshire

Meldreth Manor has earned itself a national reputation for having developed a unique multi-sensory outdoor project, 'Learning Curves'. The project was the result of collaboration between the school and a group of postgraduate students from the Art in Architecture MA course at the University of East London. Funding came from Children in Need and Allied Dunbar, as well as substantial support from parents and the local community.

The project combines art and landscape to provide a whole series of stimulatory and interactive features. The main design is a 120 metre long, fully accessible raised walkway which winds its way between the canopies of mature apple trees. A series of themed platforms include a theatre, sailing boat, rebus station, water sculptures, music instruments, a jungle walk, a slide, a 'wibbly wobbly' way, chain bridge, science platform and windmill platform.

A Scope residential special school with approximately 90 pupils. The children, aged between 5 and 19, have profound and multiple learning difficulties and associated disabilities, particularly sensory impairments and physical disabilities. The school is located in a small village and has extensive school grounds.

Outdoor design incorporates art to create an interactive, sensory rich environment.

The project opens many possibilities for creative activities and play opportunities as well as for more structured curriculum work. Children are motivated to explore and experiment and to respond to a host of different textures, sounds and sensations. There are many different opportunities for them to experience cause and effect, to be creative and to play.

The project also includes a garden area with wheelchair height planters and plants chosen for their sensory interest. A wild garden provides an enclosed, informal area with log piles and tree and shrub plantings. A pond is bordered by a wheelchair accessible path and rails which can be removed to allow pond dipping.

There are many different settings and opportunities for play including swings and roundabouts specifically designed for wheelchair users.

The school grounds are valued for their use in both the formal and informal curriculum. The grounds are used across most areas of the formal curriculum, particularly in art, science, maths and technology.

The school has been keen to regard the project as a community resource. During the summer it is open to children and parents from outside the school and there are visits from other schools.

"Grounds use permeates all aspects of school activity as a focus for and development of activities in the national curriculum".

14.5 Pitmore School, Hampshire

Pitmore School is located in an urban area adjacent to a mainstream school. The school was formerly for children with moderate learning difficulties and the present school has therefore inherited an outdoor design that was aimed at quite different types of special need. Access throughout the school, and in particular within the school grounds, is inappropriate for wheelchair users. The school grounds developments have therefore included adaptation, or removal, of inappropriate features as well as implementation of new projects. For example the original adventure playground became unsafe and had to be removed.

Outdoor projects have included the development of a new adventure playground, a pond, a minibeast area, herb garden and horticultural project. Even more than most schools, resources are a significant limiting factor as it is notoriously difficult to obtain sponsorship for this group of special needs. Only one project received help with funding and installation; the adventure playground was funded by Children in Need and constructed by Playdale. However, this was constructed before re-designation and had to be removed because it was needed for other developments.

The school grounds are used for both the formal and informal curricula and there is a strong focus on their value for social and behavioural benefits. The horticultural project includes polytunnels, greenhouses, tree and shrub production, bulb growing and cultivation of annual and perennial plants. Horticulture is valued for its variety and for the opportunities for a sense of achievement. The horticultural area is also valued as a quiet, relaxed setting for counselling and as a non-threatening environment where children can be helped to build confidence and reduce anxiety.

Grounds maintenance is a particular challenge for the school, given the limited resources. Outdoor equipment such as chairs and tables are frequently damaged by children and so there is a need for regular renewal or mending of facilities. Access to a work shop and help from the Probation Service (a group of offenders on Community Service Orders every Sunday since February 1995) have been of enormous help to the school, as was the help of the local gardening club.

> Special school for approximately 60 pupils aged between 11 and 16. All children have emotional and behavioural disorders and many have other special needs including mild and moderate learning difficulties, physical disabilities and sensory impairments.

> "The lynch pin of all outdoor activity involves new challenges in informal situations. Children who find classroom discipline impossible find outdoor activities less stressful: It allows them to release energy and tension in a relaxed, safe and controlled environment".

> "A huge variety of activities are involved, from exercising strength and ingenuity, team work (involving social skills), mutual trust and cooperation, regard for the environment, care of each other and of the plants being raised, respect for other people's achievements, personal satisfaction and success (very important if most of your experience is of failure) and even the possible future use of leisure time, work experience or work itself".

14.6 Ridgeway School and Hastingsbury School, Bedfordshire

Ridgeway School is situated on the edge of a small town, adjacent to Hastingsbury School, from which it was originally screened by a large grass mound. The grounds are extensive and, before the recent improvements, were dominated by large expanses of close mown turf and the occasional standard tree. One of the few concessions made to special needs in the original site design was a series of stark raised planters at the back of school.

The improvements were planned to increase the range of opportunities provided by the school grounds for all areas of the curriculum, to improve the appearance of the school and to encourage the integration between the two schools.

A series of projects was planned and the first addressed the walkway between the two schools. This was a purely functional straight path, very exposed and dull. The decision was taken to develop the area into a 'sensory pocket path' by incorporating areas of planting, pergolas, different surfaces and additional paths and seats. A working committee was made up of pupils from both schools and a landscape architect was commissioned to prepare a design in close collaboration with the group. The result was a successful working relationship between all involved and subsequently the development of an attractive and valuable outdoor project. The children were also involved during the construction phase. The school included a clause in the landscape specification to ensure that the planting stage would involve the children.

Special school for approximately 65 children with physical disabilities. The children cover a wide age range, 2-19, and many have associated mild learning difficulties and language disorders. Some have moderate or severe learning difficulties and/or visual impairments. Hastingsbury School is a mainstream secondary school.

"They give relevance and practical experience of all aspects of the curriculum, particularly those concerning spatial awareness, mapping skills etc."

The success of this project has meant that subsequent developments will follow a similar approach. Current attention is focused on the development of an existing overgrown copse to provide access, work stations, a pond and a bird hide. Initial clearance work was carried out primarily to get the children involved and to introduce them to the area. This was followed by classroom activities, such as drawing plans, posters etc.

The grounds are used in both the formal and informal curricula. The sensory pocket path is used for some lessons and also at break times as a social meeting place between the two schools and for integration sessions.

Other developments include an area where trees are planted as memorials to pupils who have died. This was developed to help children cope with the death of classmates and as a way of enabling families to focus their grief.

14.7　St. Ann's School, Hanwell, London

The school is located in an urban area, but benefits from several large outdoor areas which have potential as environmental classrooms. A small site fronting the school was selected as the initial project for development. This will enable visible results to be achieved within the time constraints of the project, the main aim of which was to develop an environmental garden. This would form the basis of curricular activities, be accessible to all students and staff and improve the school's appearance.

The project involved collaboration between the staff of the school and the Department of Geography at Kingston University. A final year BSc Environmental Science student designed and co-ordinated the scheme as her honours degree research project.

The design took into account existing mature trees and shrubs. Hoggin paths, edged with logs weave in and out of the vegetation, to and from a concrete path which runs down the side of the building and ends in a paved seating area. Colours, shapes and textures of plants and hard materials were used to offer as much stimulation and variety as possible. Spaces of various sizes and shapes have been created to allow for the adoption of ideas produced by the school itself.

Secondary school of 65 pupils aged 12-19 with severe and complex learning difficulties. Children's disabilities are wide ranging; many have mobility problems (including some wheelchair users), and some have sensory impairments and challenging behaviour. The school dates from the turn of the century and has been designated as a special school since 1982.

"The workdays were particularly exciting for the school because they offered the students the opportunity of working in an integrated way with people unconnected with the school. They were also able to use standard tools, such as secateurs and loppers, something they do not normally get the chance to do."

Physical labour in initial clearance was carried out by students with the help of school staff and volunteers from the local community.

The laying of the path was completed by three local volunteer groups; the Ealing group of London Wildlife Trust, Greenford Conservation in Action and Community Service Volunteers. Ealing Borough Council's Conservation Section provided some expertise, tools and labour and all materials were donated to the school. The project demonstrated the potential which could be achieved from community action and co-operation within a well designed programme of work.

The garden will become an integral part of the curriculum and form the basis of a range of themed teaching programmes. There are proposals to introduce a sculpture park, chimes in the trees, bird boxes, bird feeders, a water feature and beds for herbs. It already contains shrubs to attract birds, butterflies and other insects. Because the garden is located beside a road, making it vulnerable to vandalism, a hedge is due to be planted by the students. This will act as a natural barrier and, together with a log pile, will offer mixed habitats for the garden wildlife.

14.8 Lugton School, Dalkeith, Lothian

Lugton School has attractive grounds with extensive areas of grass, tarmac, playing fields and woodland but they provide limited opportunities for children to occupy themselves. The result has been that bullying and aggressive behaviour have developed as real problems. Plans to improve the grounds have been put in place to address these key issues. A major focus has been placed on play as this is seen as an area where more appropriate design could help encourage more purposeful activity and to reduce the level of aggressive and disruptive behaviour.

The grounds initiatives have been led by Doris Stanley, environmental studies teacher, who has been researching the use of school grounds as a teaching and learning resource as part of an MSc in Play. This has given her the opportunity to study the potential of the landscape at Lugton School for all aspects of pupils' development.

An important step was to stimulate interest and share ideas with other members of staff. An INSET day on improving the grounds, talks specific to Lugton Brae and advice from Edinburgh Wildlife Group were of great help. Two working groups of teachers and auxiliary staff were set up as the result of the support and enthusiasm of staff and this has prevented the project relying on just one person. The main activities of the working groups have been to raise funds and write policies for the school on discipline and bullying.

Special school with approximately 150 pupils between the ages of 5 and 17. The children have moderate learning difficulties and many have emotional or behavioural problems. Some also have sensory impairments, epilepsy or autism. The catchment area covers the whole of the Lothian region.

To identify potential uses of the grounds in different areas of the curriculum, Doris Stanley sent a questionnaire to all staff asking for their views and to find out if they needed work sheets and reference books to support outdoor activities. The grounds are now used in all areas of the curriculum. Several Edinburgh Arts Initiatives have been instrumental in developing outdoor art including some excellent murals and more are planned.

Over £20,000 was raised in just a year. Two murals were painted, climbing equipment and safety surfaces were installed. Toy boxes, bikes, cars and prams were purchased. An official opening ceremony of the new school grounds was held in May 1996, on LTL's National School Grounds Day, when the new Director of Education and staff, pupils and guests were entertained by the marching band of the King's Own Scottish Borderers. Plans are now well underway for more play equipment and the installation of a sensory garden in the Autumn. Nature Trails will be developed next Spring.

Maintenance is carried out by a regional council contract and the grounds changes will come under their charge. Plans are for some maintenance to be done by children and staff.

14.9 Nugent House School, Wigan

School grounds developments have focused in recent years on the development of a Horticulture Unit which is used extensively in both the formal and informal curricula. Horticulture is used for developing or maintaining a range of mental, physical and social skills. More specific emphasis is placed on particular skills including attention span and concentration, basic literacy and numeracy, listening to and responding to instructions, fine and gross motor skills and memory. The sessions are also intended to act as a forum for social interaction, discussing relevant issues and problems/successes currently being experienced.

Facilities include greenhouses, potting and storage sheds and office, a standing area for container plants and a series of beds and plots, designed for easy access and clear identification. The unit includes a production area and a more domestic garden area associated with the house. The main emphasis of the activities are fruit and vegetable production, fresh and dried flowers, bedding and flowering pot plants.

"Within its own terms horticulture has certainly provided an enjoyable and successful focus of activity as well as providing the vehicle for developing specific skills"

All the produce is used by the school, most for use in domestic science classes, preparing personal meals or for decorating classrooms, residential units and the Chapel. The pupils are also encouraged to make gifts of what they grow to family and friends. Surplus is sold to school staff but so far the unit has had no commercial pressures to be self-funding.

Residential school for boys aged between 7-19. It is part of the Nugent Care Society which works as the Welfare Agency of the Catholic Archdiocese of Liverpool, providing care for a range of vulnerable and disadvantaged people in the north west. The pupils have special educational needs associated with emotional and behavioural difficulties. The school also has a specialist unit catering for boys who require close personal support.

SOURCES OF HELP

15

15.1 Guidance on fundraising

Most school grounds projects require at least some degree of external funding. Some special schools are fortunate in having help from parents and volunteers but many have to rely on staff time. Fund-raising is time-consuming and it is therefore important not to waste time and effort through ill-prepared applications. Have clear targets (funds needed to start the project, and for further phases), make lists of materials which will be needed and take time to find out potential sources of help.

Publications that may help include the following;

A *Guide to fundraising for school grounds*, Bill Lucas and Anne Mountfield, 1995. LTL/Directory of Social Change. Provides guidance on how to fund raise. Available from Biblios, Star Road, Partridge Green, RH13 8LD 01403 710971

Directory of Grant Making Trusts. Available from the Charities Aid Foundation, 48 Pembury Road, Tonbridge, Kent TN9 2JD.

Various publications available from the Directory of Social Change, 24 Stephenson Way, London NW1 2DP Tel: 0171 284 4364.

Local firms and organisations are often a useful source of help although it can sometimes be easier to get materials rather than money.

15.2 Information on special needs

It will often be necessary to find out information specific to a particular type of disability or health issue. The following organisations provide advice and many have information packs related specifically to schools.

Action against Allergy, PO Box 278 Twickenham, TW1 4QQ.

Arthritis Care, 18 Stephenson Way, London NW1 2HD. Tel: 0171 916 1500.

Asthma Society and Friends of the Asthma Research Council, Providence House, Providence Place, London N1 0NT. Tel: 0171 226 2260. Has 'Asthma at School'.

British Diabetic Association, 10 Queen Anne Street, London W1M 0BD. Tel: 0171 323 1531.

British Epilepsy Association, Anstey House, 40 Hanover Square, Leeds LS3 1BE. Tel: 0113 2439393. Has a 'Package for Schools'.

MENCAP (Royal Society for Mentally Handicapped Children and Adults), 123 Golden Lane, London EC1Y 0RT. Tel: 0171 454 0454

MIND, Granta House, 15 - 19 Broadway, Stratford, London W15 4BQ,. Tel: 0181 519 2122.

National Eczema Society, 163 Eversholt Street, London NW1 1BU. Tel: 0171 388 4097.

Has children's information pack, including a leaflet 'Eczema at School'.

Physically Handicapped - Able-Bodied, (PHAB) Summit House, Wandle Road, Croydon, Surrey CR0 1DF. Tel: 0181 667 9443. Scotland 0131 558 9912. Wales 0122 2 22 3677. Northern Ireland 01232 796565.

Royal Association for Disability and Rehabilitation, (RADAR) Unit 2, 250 City Road, London EC1V 8AF. Tel: 0171 250 3222.

Royal National Institute for the Blind, (RNIB) 224 Great Portland St., London W1N 6AA. Tel: 0171 388 1266

Royal National Institute for the Deaf, (RNID) 19-23 Featherstone Street, London EC1Y 8SL. Tel: 0171 296 800 (voice) 0171 2296 8001 (minicom)

SCOPE, 12 Park Crescent, London W1N 4EQ. Tel: 0171 636 5020

National Autistic Society, 276 Willesdon Lane, London NW2 5RB Tel: 0181 451 1114

15.3   Information on outdoor design, use and management

There is a wide range of organisations which provide information on environmental issues relating to special needs. Additional addresses which relate to specific design issues are provided at the end of each chapter.

Access Committee for England, Unit 12 City Forum, 250 City Road, London EC1V 8AK. Tel: 0171 250 008

British Standards Institute, 389 Chiswick High Road, London W4 4AL. Tel: 0171 629 9000

Centre for Accessible Environments (CAE), Nutmeg House, 60 Gainsford St., London SE1 2NY. Tel: 0171 357 8182.

Centre for Environmental Interpretation, Metropolitan University of Manchester, Lower Chatham Street, Manchester M15 6BY. Tel: 0161 247 2000.

Countryside Commission, John Dower House, Crescent Place, Cheltenham, Glos GL50 3RA. Tel: 01242 521381.

Horticulture for All, Thorngrove Centre, Common Mead Lane, Gillingham, Dorset SP8 4RE. Tel: 01747 822242

The Fieldfare Trust, 67a The Wicker, Sheffield S3 8HT. Tel: 01742 701668.

Forestry Commission, 231 Corstorphine Road, Edinburgh EH12 7AT. Tel: 0131 334 0303.

Gardening for the Disabled Trust, The Secretary, Hayes Farmhouse, Hayes Lane, Peasmarsh, Rye, East Sussex TN31 6XR.

Horticultural Therapy, Goulds Ground, Vallis Way, Frome, Somerset BA11 3DW. Tel: 01373 464782

Learning through Landscapes, 3rd Floor, The Law Courts, Southside Offices, Winchester SO23 9DL. Tel: 01962 846258.

The National Trust, 36 Queen Ann'e Gate, London SW1H 9AS. Tel: 0171 222 5097.

Royal Society for the Protection of Birds, The Lodge, Sandy, Bedfordshire SG19 2DL. Tel: 01767 80551.

The Sensory Trust, Swindon Environment Centre, 476 Fleet Street, Swindon SN1 1RE.

Tel: 01798 526244

Water Services Association, Information Unit, 1 Queen Anne's Gate, London SW1H 9BT. Tel: 0171 222 8111.

15.4   Sources of help for construction and management work

Many schools would not be able to implement outdoor projects without the help of volunteers. The following organisations provide advice on arranging voluntary input and some have regional branches which may be able to provide practical help.

British Trust for Conservation Volunteers, 36 St Mary's Street, Wallingford, Oxon OX10 0EJ.

The National Council for Voluntary Organisations, Regents Wharf, 8 All Saints Street, London N1 9Rl. Tel: 0171 713 6161.

Community Service Volunteers, 237 Pentonville Road, London N1 9NJ. Tel: 0171 278 6601

The Wildlife Trust, WATCH, The Green, Witham Park, Waterside South, Lincoln LN5 7JR.

The Probation Service 71-73 Great Peter Street, London SW1P 2BN. Tel: 0171 222 5656.

Notes

_____

_____

_____

_____

_____

_____

_____

_____

_____

_____

_____

_____

_____

_____

_____

_____

_____

_____

_____

_____

_____

_____

_____

Notes

Notes